WINNING THE LOSER'S GAME

Timeless Strategies for Successful Investing

Charles D. Ellis

Fourth Edition

McGraw-Hill
New York Chicago San Francisco Lisbon Madrid
Mexico City Milan New Delhi San Juan
Seoul Singapore Sydney Toronto

Library of Congress Cataloging-in-Publication Data

Library of Congress Cataloging-in-Publication Data has been applied for.

McGraw-Hill

A Division of The McGraw·Hill Companies

Copyright © 2002, 1998 by Charles D. Ellis. All rights reserved. Printed in the United States of America. Except as permitted under the United States Copyright Act of 1976, no part of this publication may be reproduced or distributed in any form or by any means, or stored in a data base or retrieval system, without the prior written permission of the publisher.

1 2 3 4 5 6 7 8 9 0   DOC/DOC   0 9 8 7 6 5 4 3 2

ISBN 0-07-138767-6

This book was set in Times New Roman by North Market Street Graphics.

Printed and bound by R. R. Donnelley & Sons Company.

The second edition of this book was published in 1993 under the title *Investment Policy,* by Irwin Professional Publishing.

McGraw-Hill books are available at special quantity discounts to use as premiums and sales promotions, or for use in corporate training programs. For more information, please write to the Director of Special Sales, McGraw-Hill, 2 Penn Plaza, New York, NY 10121. Or contact your local bookstore.

This book is printed on acid-free paper.

Contents

Acknowledgments

Lucky me. My three decades as a partner in consulting at Greenwich Associates were devoted to working closely over many years with the leaders of the major investment management organizations of the United States, Australia, Canada, Japan, and Europe. Our discussions were candid, rigorous, and objective. I am forever grateful for the unique opportunity they gave me to learn about and understand investment management.

Special thanks are due to hundreds of senior investment professionals who have participated in a series of three-day seminars on investment management, sponsored by my friends and former partners at Donaldson, Lufkin, and Jenrette, which it was my great privilege to lead for 33 years. Many of the ideas in the book were developed at those seminars. Others were developed with and for the graduate students I enjoyed teaching at Harvard Business School and the Yale School of Management and the participants in AIMR's in-service course for senior professionals given each summer at Princeton. Still others crystallized during discussions with colleagues engaged in serving the worldwide professional organizations: ICFA and AIMR.

A final source of insight and learning has been my service on Yale's investment committee, particularly my discussions with David Swensen, Dean Takahashi, and Richard Levin.

One final word: I am a director of Vanguard. This book was not written because of my service to Vanguard: it's the other way around. I was pleased and proud to join Vanguard because that remarkable organization is clearly devoted to serving investors who are ready for and interested in winning investing.

Friends who have given generously of their time and understanding to help me include Linda Koch Lorimer, Chad Ellis, Harold Ellis, Claude Rosenberg, Jason Zweig, Jonathan Clements, Dero Saunders, Tad Jeffrey, Rosalind Whitehead, Dean LeBaron, Paul Bordeau, and Yuji Kage. Shirley Cacace did all the typing.

Charles D. Ellis
New Haven

Foreword

"IT'S DIFFERENT THIS TIME." Those four words began to circulate through the investment community and the popular media late in the great bull market of the 1980s and 1990s. As a frenzy developed over growth stocks and the supposed dot.com revolution, investing became Americans' new national pastime. Professional investors and amateurs alike were beguiled by the notion that old rules about investing were invalidated by a new economic paradigm. Who cared about balance, diversification, and investing for the long term?

But it *wasn't* different this time. As has happened so often in the past, the market proved again the folly of imprudent investing and reckless speculation. For many, it was a painful lesson. Trillions of dollars were lost in the markets with the bursting of the speculative bubble in the spring of 2000.

With hard lessons at hand, it's always useful to take a fresh look at wisdom that has stood the test of time. *Winning the Loser's Game* is just such a resource. This book, which grew out of Charley Ellis's insightful and provocative 1975 *Financial Analysts Journal* article on the folly of trying to beat the markets, has served as a primer and a touchstone for investors since it was first published in 1985. Though the book's premise may have seemed unconventional in 1975, its wisdom has been borne out again and again. To this day, that article remains in my view one of the most comprehensive, pragmatic, and interesting pieces on investments ever written. I know I have returned to Charley Ellis's insights many times over the years and discovered new meaning in every new reading.

I first encountered the wisdom of Charley Ellis when I was an MBA student in 1980. His 1975 article, entitled "The Loser's Game," was assigned reading for my investment-management class. I remember picking up the article and thinking it probably wouldn't tell me anything that I didn't already know. What a surprise awaited me.

Here, in matter-of-fact language—terms that even a self-confident MBA student could appreciate—was a compelling explanation of how investment management had evolved from a winner's game to a loser's game. In the 1970s, as the industry became dominated by institutional investors, the odds against outperforming the market had become much more formidable. The author compared investing to another loser's game— amateur tennis—where the victor is typically the player who makes fewer errors, not the player who tries to deliver brilliant serves.

In 1982, when I made a career change from manufacturing to money management and joined Vanguard, one of my new colleagues welcomed me to the company by giving me another copy of the famous Ellis article. As a champion of index investing, Vanguard has given investors a new weapon in the "loser's game." Index funds seek to match, not beat, the performance of the market, and, with time, the cost advantage of that passive approach translates into a powerful performance advantage.

But this time, I also read the essay from the point of view of an industry participant. What resonated most was the author's straightforward appraisal of the investment industry's failings. With its unique corporate structure as a mutual organization, however, Vanguard had been designed on the premise that a better form of mutual fund company could win the loser's game. An investment management firm could achieve a powerful and sustainable long-term competitive advantage by championing a disciplined, sensible approach to investing and by putting the needs of its clients first. We began to tap into Charley's consulting expertise through Greenwich Associates, the international business-strategy consulting firm he had founded in 1972.

Given our shared views on investing, Charley Ellis and Vanguard were bound to forge an official alliance sooner or later. To my delight, the connection was formalized in 2001, when we were able to recruit him for Vanguard's board of directors upon his retirement from Greenwich Associates. Now, I'm fortunate to be able to call upon his expertise regularly on behalf of millions of Vanguard investors. Having been influenced by his thinking from afar for so long, I appreciate having the benefit of his experience and perspective up close.

One of the most important and enduring aspects of *Winning the Loser's Game* has been its broad applicability to anyone involved with investments. That's particularly true of this fourth edition, which has five new chapters, including new material on the advantages of index funds.

- Professional investors (or those who aspire to become professionals) will find a clear articulation of the challenges that must be overcome to succeed. In a word, it provides humility.

- Fiduciaries will find a road map for overseeing important pools of capital to ensure that goals and objectives are achieved.

- Individual investors will find time-tested practical advice as well as the big picture—a valuable resource that can provide a "reality check" in all investment environments.

Since the 1975 publication of "The Loser's Game," the investment industry has undergone a momentous transformation. Back then, the individual retirement account was just coming on the scene. The 401(k) retirement plan hadn't been invented. But in the next decade, a remarkable thing occurred: Because of IRAs and 401(k)s, together with the long-running bull market in stocks, millions of Americans discovered the rewards of long-term investing. American investors have an estimated $2.7 trillion in IRAs (46 percent of it in mutual funds) and another $1.7 trillion in 401(k) plans (45 percent through mutual funds) as of year-end 2000. Total assets invested in mutual funds by individual and institutional investors—including both retirement and nonretirement assets—stood at nearly $7 trillion at the end of 2000.

At the heart of this phenomenal growth is the simple notion of financial empowerment. Individuals *can* take responsibility for their own financial well-being through disciplined investing. Whether the goal is to tuck away savings for a child's college education or for retirement or for some other long-term need, success rests on a simple and sensible approach: Construct a prudent, well-diversified plan that suits your individual goals, time horizon, and risk tolerance and that minimizes your costs—and then stick to it. Disciplined investors have the confidence and perspective to endure the market's inevitable downturns. They probably also sleep better at night than the investors who feverishly buy and sell funds or individual securities in a fruitless effort to beat the markets. Most important, in the end, they are more successful at building wealth.

There will always be times when an investor is tempted to abandon the fundamental principles of investing and give in to greed—or fear. That's just what we saw in the speculative stock market bubble of the 1990s and in the backlash after the bubble burst, when irrational fear drove some long-term investors to flee the stock market. *Winning the Loser's Game* takes a balanced, realistic view of the risks and rewards of investing, and that's why it's ultimately so useful for individual investors who are struggling to make sense of recent history.

Bookstore shelves are crowded with books on investing, but in my view, just a few of them are truly must-reads. Having recommended previous editions of *Winning the Loser's Game* to many business students, new Vanguard crew members, and personal friends over the years, I am pleased to recommend this new must-read to you.

John J. Brennan
Malvern, Pennsylvania
January 14, 2002

For Linda Koch Lorimer, my beloved wife and best friend. You helped me learn that striving to maximize quantitative investment results was not as important as assuring financial security and the freedom to enjoy living well comfortably.

CHAPTER 1

THE LOSER'S GAME

DISAGREEABLE DATA ARE STREAMING STEADILY out of the computers of performance measurement firms. Over and over again these facts and figures inform us that investment managers are failing to "perform," that is, to beat the market. Occasional periods of above-average results raise expectations that are soon dashed as false hopes. Contrary to their often articulated goal of outperforming the market averages, the nation's professional investment managers are not beating the market; the market is beating them.

Faced with information that contradicts what they believe, people tend to respond in one of two ways. Some ignore the new knowledge and hold to their former beliefs. Others accept the validity of the new information, factor it into their perception of reality, and put it to use.

Investment management, as traditionally practiced, is based on a single basic belief: Professional investment managers *can* beat the market. That premise appears to be false (see Figure 1-1).

If the premise that it is feasible to outperform the market were true, then deciding *how* to go about achieving success would be a matter of straightforward logic.

First, since the overall market can be represented by a passive and public listing such as the Standard & Poor's 500 Stock Index (S&P 500), a successful manager need only rearrange his or her portfolios more produc-

3

FIGURE 1-1   Performance of general equity funds outperformed by the S&P 500, 1963–2001.

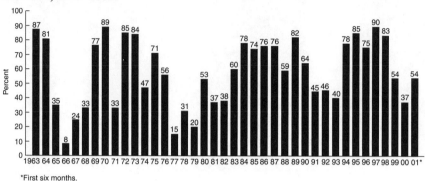

*First six months.

tively than the "mindless" S&P 500. The manager can be different in stock selection, strategic emphasis on particular groups of stocks, market timing, or various combinations of these strategies.

Second, since an active manager wants to make as many "right" decisions as possible, he or she will assemble a group of bright, well-educated, highly motivated, hardworking professionals whose collective purpose will be to identify underpriced securities to buy overpriced securities to sell—and to beat the market by shrewdly betting against the crowd.

Investment managers are not beating the market; the market is beating them.

Unhappily, the basic assumption that most institutional investors can outperform the market is false. The institutions *are* the market. They cannot, as a group, outperform themselves. In fact, given the cost of active management—fees, commissions, market impact of transactions, and so forth—75 percent of investment managers have and will over the long term underperform the overall market.

Because investing institutions are so numerous and capable and determined to do well for their clients, investment management is not a "winner's game." It has become a loser's game. Day-trading is worse: It is a sucker's game. Don't do it—ever.

Before analyzing what happened to convert institutional investing from a winner's game to a loser's game, consider the profound difference between these two kinds of games. In a winner's game the outcome is determined by the correct actions of the *winner*. In a loser's game, the outcome is determined by mistakes made by the *loser*.

Dr. Simon Ramo, a scientist at TRW Inc., identified the crucial difference between a winner's game and a loser's game in an excellent book on playing strategy, *Extraordinary Tennis for the Ordinary Tennis Player*.[1] Over many years Dr. Ramo observed that tennis is not one game but two: one played by professionals and a very few gifted amateurs, the other played by all the rest of us.

Investing has changed from a winner's game to a loser's game.

Although players in both games use the same equipment, dress, rules, and scoring and conform to the same etiquette and customs, they play two very different games. After extensive scientific and statistical analysis, Ramo summed it up this way: Professionals *win* points; amateurs *lose* points.

In expert tennis the ultimate outcome is determined by the actions of the *winner*. Professional tennis players stroke the ball hard, with laserlike precision, through long and often exciting rallies until one player is able to drive the ball just out of reach or force the other player to make an error. These splendid players seldom make mistakes.

Amateur tennis, Ramo found, is almost entirely different. The outcome is determined by the loser. Here's how. Brilliant shots, long and exciting rallies, and seemingly miraculous recoveries are few and far between. Instead, the ball often is hit into the net or out of bounds, and double faults at service are not uncommon. The amateur seldom beats the *opponent* but instead beats *himself* all the time. The victor in this game of tennis gets a higher score *because her opponent is losing even more points*. Instead of trying to add power to our serve or hit closer to the line, we should concentrate on consistency and getting the ball back.

As a scientist and statistician, Ramo gathered data to test his hypothesis in a clever way. Instead of keeping conventional game scores—love, 15 all, 30–15, and so forth—Ramo simply counted points won versus points lost. He found that in expert tennis about 80 percent of the points are won, whereas in amateur tennis about 80 percent of the points are lost.

---

[1] Simon Ramo, *Extraordinary Tennis for the Ordinary Tennis Player* (New York: Crown Publishers, 1977).

The two games are fundamental opposites. Professional tennis is a winner's game: The outcome is determined by the actions of the winner. Amateur tennis is a loser's game: The outcome is determined by the actions of the loser, who defeats himself.

The distinguished military historian Admiral Samuel Elliot Morison makes a similar central point in his thoughtful treatise *Strategy and Compromise:* "In warfare, mistakes are inevitable. Military decisions are based on estimates of the enemy's strengths and intentions that are usually faulty, and on intelligence that is never complete and often misleading. Other things being equal," concludes Morison, "the side that makes the fewest strategic errors wins the war."[2]

War is the ultimate loser's game. Amateur golf is another. Tommy Armour in his book *How to Play Your Best Golf All the Time* says: "The best way to win is by making fewer bad shots,"[3] an observation with which all weekend golfers would concur. There are many other loser's games. Some, like institutional investing, were once winner's games but have changed into loser's games with the passage of time. For example, 70 or 80 years ago only very brave, athletic, strong-willed young people with good eyesight had the nerve to try flying an airplane. In those glorious days, flying was a winner's game. But times have changed, and so has flying. If the pilot of your 747 came aboard today wearing a 50-mission hat and a long white silk scarf around his or her neck, you'd get off. Such people no longer belong in airplanes because flying today is a loser's game with one simple rule: Don't make mistakes.

Likewise, the "money game" we call investment management has evolved in recent decades from a winner's game to a loser's game.[4] A basic change has occurred in the investment environment; the market came to be dominated in the 1970s by the very institutions that were striving to win by outperforming the market. In just 40 years the market activities of the investing institutions shifted from only 10 percent of total public transactions to an overwhelming 90 percent. And that shift made all the difference. No longer was the active investment manager competing with cautious custodians or amateurs who were out of touch with the market: Now he or she

---

[2]Samuel Elliot Morison, *Strategy and Compromise* (New York: Little Brown, 1958).

[3]Tommy Armour, *How to Play Your Best Golf All the Time* (New York: Simon & Schuster, 1971).

[4]Perhaps winner's games self-destruct because they attract too many players, all of whom want to win. (That's why gold rushes finish ugly.)

was competing with other experts in a loser's game where the secret to winning is to lose less than the others lose.

The money game includes a formidable group of competitors. At least 200 major institutional investors and another 1,000 small- and medium-size institutions operate in the market all day, every day, in the most intensely competitive way. The 50 largest, most active institutions do fully 50 percent of all the trades in the market. Thus, about half the time we buy and about half the time we sell, the "other fellow" is one of these giant professionals, with all their resources.

The key question under the new rules of the game is this: How much better must the active manager be to *at least* recover the costs of active management? The answer is daunting. If we assume 80 percent portfolio turnover (implying that the fund manager holds a typical stock for 15 months, which is approximately average for the fund industry) and total trading costs (commission plus the "spread") of 1 percent to buy and 1 percent to sell (again, average rates), plus a fee for active management of 1.25 percent (slightly below the average among U.S. stock mutual funds), the typical fund's operating costs are 2.85 percent per year.[5]

Recovering these costs is surprisingly difficult in a market dominated by professional investors who are very competitive, extraordinarily well informed, and continuously active and make few large mistakes and, when they do make mistakes, correct their errors quickly *or* see them exploited (and quickly corrected) by their professional competitors. For example, assuming an average annual rate of return of 10 percent for stocks, an active manager must overcome the drag of 2.85 percent from annual operating costs. If the fund manager is only to match the market's 10 percent return after all costs, he or she must return 12.85 percent before his or her costs. In other words, for you merely to do as well as the market, your fund manager must be able to outperform it by 28.5 percent![6]

---

[5] (1.25 percent + 0.80 × [1 percent + 1 percent]). Far more than brokerage commissions and dealer spreads are properly included in transactions costs. The best way to show how high transactions costs are is to compare the *theoretical* results of a "paper portfolio" with the *actual* results of a "real money portfolio." Experts will tell you the differences are always impressive. And there's yet another cost of transactions—the cost of unwisely getting into stocks you would not have purchased if you were not "sure" you could get out at any time because the market looks so liquid. This is a real liquidity trap. Think how differently people would behave on the highway or in the bedroom if they were not so sure they would not be caught. It's the same way in investments: You don't always get caught, nor do you always *not* get caught. *All* these costs are part of the *total transactions costs*.

[6] Which makes the sustained superior performance of Warren Buffet so wonderful.

The stark reality is that most money managers have been losing the money game. The historical record is that on a cumulative basis, over three-quarters of professionally managed funds *under*performed the S&P 500 Market Stock Average.

Thus, the burden of proof is on the person who says, "I am a winner; I can win the money game." Because only a sucker backs a false "winner" in a loser's game, investors have a right to demand that an investment manager explain exactly what he or she is going to do and why it is going to work so well.

If investment managers are on balance not beating the market, investors should at least consider joining it by investing in passive index funds that replicate the market. The data from the performance measurement firms suggest that an index fund would have outperformed most investment managers over long periods of time.

The reason that investing has become a loser's game, especially for the professionals who manage the leading mutual funds and investment management organizations, is that in the complex problem each manager is trying to solve, his or her efforts and the efforts of his or her many determined competitors to find a solution have become the dominant variables. And their efforts to beat the market are no longer the most important part of the solution; they are the most important part of the problem.

For any one manager to outperform the other professionals, she must be so skillful and so quick that she can regularly catch other professionals making errors—and can systematically exploit those errors faster than other professionals can. Working *efficiently,* as Peter Drucker has explained, means knowing how to do things the right way, but working *effectively* means doing the right things. Investment counseling helps investors do the right things. The investment counselor's main professional task is to help each client identify, understand, and commit consistently and continually to long-term investment objectives that are both realistic in the capital markets and appropriate to the objectives of the client.

The hardest part of the work is not figuring out the optimal investment policy; it is staying committed to sound investment policy and maintaining what Disraeli called "constancy to purpose." Sustaining a long-term focus at market highs or market lows is notoriously hard. In either case, emotions are strongest and current market action appears most demanding of change because the apparent "facts" seem most compelling. This is why being rational in an emotional environment is not easy. Holding on to a sound policy through thick and thin is extraordinarily difficult *and* extraordinarily important work. This is why investors can benefit from sound investment. The cost of infidelity can be very high.

The main reason managers' results are so disappointing is that the competitive environment within which they work has changed in just 30 years from quite favorable to very adverse, and it is getting worse and worse. (Those inclined to dismiss dinosaurs should remember that those great beasts roamed the earth for a very long time—over 100 million years—before *their* climate changed from favorable to adverse.)

Before examining the changes in the investment climate, let's remind ourselves that active investing is at the margin always a negative-sum game. Changing investments among investors would by itself be a zero-sum game, but costs such as commissions, expenses, and market impact must be deducted. Net result: a negative-sum game.

To achieve superior or better than average results through active management, you depend directly on exploiting the mistakes and blunders of others. Others must be acting as though they were *willing to lose* so that you can *win*—after covering all your costs of operation. In the 1960s, when institutions did only 10 percent of the public trading on the New York Stock Exchange (NYSE) and individual investors did 90 percent, large numbers of amateurs were realistically bound to lose to the professionals. We can understand why this was the reality of the situation by reviewing some of the characteristics of individual investors.

Individual investors buy for reasons *outside* the stock market: They buy because they inherit money, get a bonus, sell a house, or, for any other happy reason, have money to invest as a result of something that has no direct connection to the stock market. They sell stocks because a child is going off to college or they have decided to buy a home—almost always for reasons *outside* the stock market.

In addition, individual investors typically do not do extensive, rigorous comparison shopping across the many alternatives *within* the stock market. Most individual investors are not experts on even a few companies. Many rely for information on newspapers, television, friends, or retail stockbrokers—who are seldom experts. Individuals may *think* they know something important when they invest, but almost always what they think they know either is not true or is not relevant or not important (because it is already known and has already been factored into the market price by the professionals who are active in the market all the time). Thus, the activity of most individual investors is what market researchers correctly call "informationless" trading. (This term is descriptive. Anyone who feels offended is too personally sensitive.)

It is little wonder that back in the 1960s professional investors—who are always working *inside* the market, making rigorous comparisons of price to value across hundreds and hundreds of different stocks on which they can command extensive, up-to-the-minute information—thought they would outperform the individual investors who dominated the stock market and did 90 percent of all the trading. Back then the professionals could and did outperform the amateurs. But that was over a generation ago.

The picture is profoundly different now. After 40 years of enormous growth in mutual funds, pension funds, and hedge funds *and* increasing turnover in those institutions' portfolios, the old 90:10 ratio has been *completely* reversed. Today 90 percent of all NYSE "public" trades are made by investment professionals. In fact, 75 percent of all trading is done by the professionals at the 100 largest and most active institutions, and 50 percent of all NYSE trading is done by the professionals at the 50 largest and most active institutional investors.

And what tough professionals they are! Top of their class in college and at graduate school, they are "the best and the brightest"—disciplined and rational, supplied with extraordinary information by thousands of analysts who are highly motivated, very hardworking, and very competitive—and all playing to *win*. Sure, professionals make errors and mistakes, but the other pros are always looking for any error and will pounce on it as quickly as they can. Attractive investment opportunities simply don't come along often, and the few that do don't last very long. Yes, some professionals beat the market in any particular year or in any decade, but scrutiny of the records reveals that very few professionals beat the market averages over the long haul.

Even more discouraging to investors searching for superior managers, those managers who have had superior results in the *past* are unlikely to have superior results in the *future*. In investment performance, the past is *not* prologue. Regression to the mean (the tendency for behavior to move toward "normal" or average) is a persistently powerful phenomenon in physics and sociology—and in investing. Thus, many professional investment managers are so good, they make it nearly impossible for any one professional to outperform the market they together now dominate.

The exciting truth is that while most investors are doomed to lose if they play the loser's game of trying to beat the market, every investor can be a winner. All we need to do to be long-term winners is to reorient ourselves and concentrate on realistic long-term goal setting, sound policies to achieve our goals, and the requisite self-discipline, patience, and fortitude required for persistent implementation.

2

BEATING THE MARKET

THE ONLY WAY TO BEAT THE MARKET, after adjusting for market risk, is to discover and exploit other investors' mistakes.

It can be done, and it has been done by most investors some of the time. However, very few investors have been able to outsmart and outmaneuver other investors often enough to beat the market consistently over the long term.

Active investment managers can try to succeed on any or all of four investment vectors:

1. Market timing
2. Selection of specific stocks or groups of stocks
3. Changes in portfolio structure or strategy
4. An insightful, long-term investment concept or philosophy

Even the most casual observer of markets and securities will be impressed by the splendid array of apparent opportunities to do better than "settle for average." The price charts for the overall market, for major industry groups, and for individual stocks make it seem deceptively "obvious" that active investors can do better. After all, we can see with our own eyes that the stars perform consistently better than "average" in fields such as sports, theater, and medicine, so why not in investing? Why shouldn't many investment managers also be consistently above average? In short, why should it be so hard to beat the market?

The most audacious way to increase potential returns is through market timing. The classic market timer moves the portfolio in and out of the market so that it is, she hopes, fully invested during rising markets and out of the market when prices are falling. Another form of timing would shift an equity portfolio out of stock groups that are expected to underperform the market and into groups that may outperform it. Remember, every time you decide to get out of the market (*or* get in), the investors you buy from (or sell to) are the best of the big professionals. (Of course, they're not *always* right, but how confident are you that you will be "more right" more often than they will be?) What's more, you will incur trading costs or mutual fund sales charges with each and every move. And unless you are managing a tax-sheltered retirement account, you will have to pay taxes every time you take a profit.

In a bond portfolio the market timer hopes to shift into long maturities before falling interest rates drive up long bond prices and back into short maturities before rising interest rates drive down long bond prices.

The only way to beat the market is to exploit other investors' mistakes.

In a balanced portfolio, the market timer strives to invest more heavily in stocks when they will produce greater total returns than bonds, then shift into bonds when they will produce greater total returns than equities, and then into short-term investments when they will produce greater total returns than either bonds or stocks.

A delightful comparative analysis of two kinds of investment perfection for the period 1940–1973 gives a sense of the seductive "potential" of market timing. The first record was the result of perfect market timing with 100 percent in stocks in all rising markets and 100 percent in cash in all falling markets.

With 22 transactions (11 buys and 11 sells) in 34 years, and using the Dow Jones Industrial Average as a proxy for stocks, $1,000 was expanded into $85,937.

During the same 34-year period, with the hypothetical portfolio always 100 percent invested and always invested in the one best industry group, the same $1,000 (with 28 buys and 28 sells) exploded into $4,357,000,000!

The last two years indicate the pluck requisite to the process: In January 1971, $687 million was invested in restaurant companies; it became $1.7 billion by year end and was then committed to gold stocks, which carried it up to $4.4 billion by Christmas! Of course this example is absurd. It has never been done and never will be done.

Despite the enticing appeal of reducing market exposure by means of astute sales when securities appear to be overpriced and by boldly reinvesting when prices appear to have declined to attractive low levels—selling high and buying low—the overwhelming evidence shows that market timing is not an effective way to increase returns for one dour but compelling reason: on average and over time, *it does not work.* Market timing does not work because no manager is so much more astute than his or her professional competitors on a repetitive basis and because so much of the stock market "action" occurs in such brief periods and at times when investors are most likely to be captives of a conventional consensus.

The market does just as well, on average, when the investor is *out* of the market as it does when he is *in* it. Therefore, the investor loses money relative to a simple buy-and-hold strategy by being out of the market part of the time.

Perhaps the best insight into the difficulties of market timing came from an experienced professional's candid lament: "I've seen lots of interesting approaches to market timing—and I have tried most of them in my 40 years of investing. They may have been great before my time, but not one of them worked for me. Not one!"

Just as there are *old* pilots and *bold* pilots, there are no old, bold pilots; likewise, there are *no* investors who have achieved recurring successes in market timing. Decisions that are driven by greed or fear are usually wrong, usually late, and very unlikely to be reversed correctly. Particularly with real money, don't even *consider* trying to outguess the market or outmaneuver the professionals to "sell high" and "buy low." You'll fail, perhaps disastrously.

Another reason is even more striking. Figure 2-1 shows what happens to long-term compound returns when the best days are removed from the record. Taking out the 10 best days—less than ¼ of 1 percent of the period examined—cuts the average rate of return by 17 percent (from 18 percent to 15 percent). Taking the 10 next best days away cuts returns to 13.1 percent. Removing a total of 30 days—just ½ percent of the total period—cuts returns almost 40 percent, from 18 percent to 11 percent. Figure 2-2 shows a similar result when the best *years* are excluded from the calculation of the long-term averages.

FIGURE 2-1   Compound returns (%), 1982–2000.
Courtesy of Cambridge Associates.

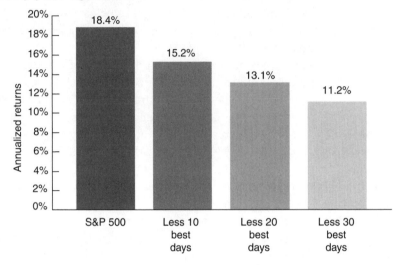

Market timing is a "wicked" idea.
Don't try it—ever.

Using the S&P 500 average returns, the story is told quickly and clearly: All the total returns on stocks in the past 75 years were achieved in the best 60 *months*—less than 7 percent of those 800 months—over those long years. (Imagine the profits if we could know which months! But we cannot and will not.) What we do know is both simple and valuable: If we missed those few and fabulous 60 best months, we would have missed almost all the total returns accumulated over two full generations. A recent study by T. Rowe Price shows that a $1 investment in the S&P 500 that missed the 90 best trading days in the 10 years from June 30, 1989, to June 30, 1999, would have *lost* money (22 cents) and would have made only 30 cents if it missed the best 60 days—but would have made $5.59 by staying fully invested. (Seductively, for those willing to be seduced, sidestepping the 90 worst trading days would have resulted in a 10-year gain of $42.78.) Removing just the five best *days* out of 72 *years* of investing reduces cumulative compound returns—without dividend investments—by nearly 50

FIGURE 2-2   Cumulative returns on one dollar invested, 1928–2000.
Courtesy of Cambridge Associates, Datastream International, and McGraw-Hill.

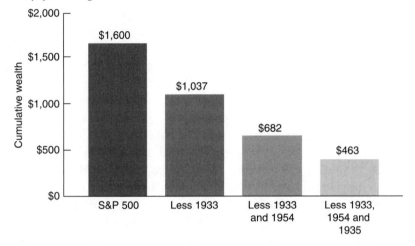

percent.[1] That's why most "active" investors should carefully consider Mies van der Rohe's admonition on architecture: "Less is more." The lesson is clear: You have to be there "when lightning strikes." That's why market timing is, as we've said, a truly "wicked" idea. Don't try it—ever.

The second tactical way to increase returns is through stock selection, or "stock picking." Professional investors devote an extraordinary amount of skill, time, and effort to this work. Stock valuation dominates the research efforts of investing institutions and the research services of stockbrokers.

Through financial analysis or field studies of competitors and suppliers as well as management interviews, investors seek to attain a better understanding of the investment value of a security or a group of securities than the market consensus. When investment managers find significant differences between the market price and the value of a security (as they appraise it), they can buy or sell as appropriate to capture the differential

[1]On Wall Street, the coming of summer is marked with stories about the summer rally, the fall is heralded by laments about October being the worst month for stocks (statistically it is actually September), and the turn of the year is celebrated with the January effect—which may not always arrive but rarely comes in November. Mark Twain's comments about the stock market may have said it best: "October. This is one of the peculiarly dangerous months to speculate stocks in. The others are July, January, September, April, November, May, March, June, December, August and February." (*Puddin'head Wilson,* 1893).

between the market's price and the true investment value for their clients' portfolios.

Unfortunately, however, security analysis taken as a whole does not appear to be a useful or profitable activity. The stocks investment managers sell after doing fundamental research and the stocks they don't buy typically do as well as the stocks they do buy (because they sell from each other and buy from each other, making the market "efficient").

Again, the problem is not that investment research is not done well. The problem is that it is done so well by so many—particularly by the research analysts at major brokerage firms, who share their information and evaluations almost instantly through global information networks with hundreds of professional investors who take swift reactive action, often striving to act quickly in anticipation of how others will soon act—that no single group of investors is likely to gain a regular and repetitive useful advantage over all other investors. And the only way to beat the market is to beat the other professionals who, as a group, *are* the market—and particularly, as we'll soon see, outperform the 50 most active institutions.

Strategic decisions in both stock and bond portfolios involve major commitments that affect the overall structure of the portfolio. They are made to exploit insights into major industry groups, changes in the economy and interest rates, or anticipated shifts in the valuation of major types of stocks, such as "emerging growth" stocks and "basic industry" stocks. Each of these judgments involves what can be described as market segment risk.

For example, in the late 1990s, those investors who were most committed to Internet technology enjoyed a wonderful run-up romp—until the sharp market "correction" in 2000. "The market giveth, and the market taketh away!" In the 1980s portfolio managers who invested heavily in two areas—oil and technology—had very favorable results compared to investors who chose instead to invest heavily in utilities and other interest-sensitive stocks or in consumer stocks. Equally important, they had to be out of energy stocks in 1981 or they would have had to "give it all back."

In the early 1970s, portfolio managers who invested heavily in large-capitalization growth stocks—the "Nifty 50"—experienced exceptionally favorable results as the notorious "two tier" market developed.[2] In the later 1970s the same securities produced exceptionally negative results

---

[2] Growth stocks had a much higher price/earnings (P/E) ratio than industrial stocks, dividing the market into two tiers.

when previously anticipated earnings failed to materialize and institutions became disenchanted with the concept and dumped their holdings, collapsing the price/earnings ratios and driving stock prices way down. The same up, up, up—*down* phenomenon has been repeated many times. All too often, at the peak the articulated consensus is "This time it's different!"

As the well-worn saying goes, it is not a stock market but a market of stocks—one that lures portfolio managers (but not without peril) to make major strategic decisions on groups of stocks in the portfolios they manage.

Full of interesting potential—being in the right place at the right time—this approach to investing challenges the manager to discover a new (and often unfamiliar) way to invest as markets shift, become proficient at each new way, and then abandon it for another new way. In theory, of course, this can be done, but *will* it be done? By which managers? For how long?

The fourth possible way to increase returns is to develop a profound and valid insight into the forces that drive a particular sector of the market or a particular group of companies or industries and systematically exploit that investment insight or concept.

Investing to exploit an enduring investment concept or philosophy involves an enduring investment commitment—through cycle after cycle in the stock market and in the business economy—for an individual portfolio manager or an entire investment management organization.

An organization that is committed, for example, to growth-stock investing will concentrate on evaluating new technologies, understanding the management skills required to lead rapidly growing organizations, and analyzing the financial requirements for investing in new markets and new products to sustain growth. This type of investment organization should learn from experience—sometimes painful experience—how to discriminate between ersatz "growth stocks" that fizzle out and true growth companies that will achieve success over many years.

Other investment management organizations take the view that among the many large corporations in mature and often cyclical industries, there are always some that have considerably greater investment value than is recognized by other investors; that with astute research, these superior values can be isolated; and that by buying good values at depressed prices, these investment managers can achieve superior returns for their clients with relatively low risk. Such organizations develop considerable expertise in "separating the wheat from the chaff," avoiding the low-priced stocks that *ought* to be low-priced and ferreting out insights into investment value that other investors have not yet recognized.

The important test of an investment concept or philosophy is the manager's ability to adhere to it persistently for valid, long-term reasons even when the short-term results are disagreeable and disheartening. Persistence can lead to mastery of an important distinctive competence in the particular kind of investing in which a manager specializes.

The great advantage of the conceptual or philosophical approach is that the investment firm can organize itself to do its own particular kind of investing all the time, avoid the noise and confusion of alternatives, attract investment analysts and managers interested in and skilled at the particular type of investing, and through continuous practice, self-critique, and study master it. The great disadvantage is that if the chosen kind of investing becomes obsolete, overpriced, or out of touch with the changing market, a proficient specialist organization is most unlikely to detect the need for change until it is too late for its clients and itself.

What is remarkable about these profound investment concepts is how few have been discovered that last for very long—most likely because the hallmark of a free capital market is that few if any opportunities to establish a proprietary long-term competitive advantage can be found and maintained for a long time.

All four of these basic forms of active investing have one fundamental characteristic in common: *They depend on the errors of others.* Whether by omission or commission, the only way in which a profit opportunity can be available to an active investor—in an individual stock or a group of stocks—is that the consensus of other professional investors is *wrong.* While this sort of collective error does occur, we must ask how often these errors are made and how often any manager could avoid making the same errors and instead have the wisdom and courage to take action opposed to the consensus!

With so many competitors seeking superior insight into the value/price relationship of individual stocks or industry groups and with so much information so widely and rapidly communicated throughout the investment community, the chances of discovering and exploiting profitable insights into individual stocks or groups of stocks—opportunities left behind by the errors and inattention of other investors—are certainly not richly promising.

One way to increase success in lifelong investing is to reduce and remove errors. (Ask any golfer or tennis player.) Here's a mistake many investors make: trying too hard—striving to get more from investments or investment managers than they can repetitively produce. Trying too hard—and thus courting disappointment—is all too often eventually expensive because taking too much risk *is* too much risk.[3]

Another mistake individual investors all too often make is not trying hard enough—usually by being cautious for short-term reasons when successful investing requires long-term thinking and long-term behavior. Being too defensive can be expensive. For example, during the past two decades it has been costly to hold even a modest cash reserve within an equity portfolio or to concentrate bond investments on U.S. governments (instead of using such alternatives as GNMA pass-throughs).

With so many apparent opportunities to do better than the market, it must be disconcerting for investors to see—and difficult to accept—how hard it is to do better than the market after an adjustment for risks[4] over the long haul. Yet even the most talented investment manager must wonder how he can expect his hardworking and determined competitors to provide him—through incompetence, error, or inattention—with sufficiently attractive opportunities to buy or sell in size on significantly advantageous terms on such a regular basis that he can "beat the market" by beating them.

In the movie *Full Metal Jacket* two drill sergeants are watching their basic training class jogging in close-order drill to their graduation ceremony, shouting military calls like "Airborne! All the way!" One drill sergeant says, "Sarge, what do you see when you look at those boys?" After

[3] In a paper entitled "Why *Do* Investors Trade Too Much?" Terrance Odean, finance professor at the University of California at Davis, looked at nearly 100,000 stock trades made by retail investors at a major discount brokerage firm from 1987 through 1993. He found that on average the stocks these investors bought underperformed the market by 2.7 percentage points over the following year, while the stocks they sold outperformed the market by 0.5 point in the following year. Similarly, in a paper published by Brookings Institution, economists Josef Lakonishok, Andrei Shleifer, and Robert Vishny showed that the stock trades made by professional fund managers subtracted 0.78 percent from the returns they would have earned by keeping their portfolios constant. Finally, the Plexus Group, a consulting firm that researches the costs of trading for professional money managers, studied more than 80,000 trades by 19 investment firms and found that the typical purchase of a stock added 0.67 percent to a fund's short-term return but that the typical sale subtracted 1.08 percent. No wonder Philip Caret, the 100-year-old founder of the Pioneer Fund, said, "Turnover usually indicates a failure of judgment. It's extremely difficult to figure out when to sell anything."

[4] See Chapter 1 for an explanation.

the classic expectoration, the other man replies, "What do I see? I'll tell yeh. About 10 percent of those boys are honest to God *real* soldiers!" Pause. "The rest . . . are just . . . targets!" That's just a scene from a war flick, but it may have real life meaning for you. For example, just how good are you as an investor? Here's a way to turn on the lights.

Let's assume that you are so skilled and so well informed that you are in fact in the top 10 percent of all individual investors. Bravo! Take a bow— but watch out!

Here's why. Even if you are a far *above* average investor, you are almost certain to be making *below*-average investments. It's in the numbers. The first step into reality is to recognize that the key is *not* the skill and knowledge of the *investor* but the skill and knowledge with which each specific investment *transaction* is made. The second step is to recognize and accept the reality that fully one-half of all the trades on the NYSE are made by the 50 largest and most active institutional investors.

Just how good and tough to beat is the fiftieth largest institution? Here are some realities: The fiftieth institution[5] pays Wall Street over $50 *million* in commissions every year for information and insight so that it can call on any analyst at any stockbroker at any time and get immediate full service. It also gets a constant stream of hundreds and hundreds of incoming "first calls" every day from Wall Street. It has Bloomberg and all the other sophisticated information services. Its professionals meet with corporate managements frequently. It has a team of in-house analysts and a group of senior portfolio managers—50 to 100 professionals with an average of 20 years of investing experience—all working their contacts and networks to get the best information all the time. You get the picture: The fiftieth institution has all the advantages.

Chances are, *none* of us can beat *any* of the 50 largest institutions on a regular basis—or the next 50 largest institutions. These 100 largest institutional investors execute 75 percent of all the trades each day on the NYSE. Given this reality, the *best* individual investors are virtually certain to be confined to executing investment transactions that are in only the fourth quartile of all transactions. That's why even if you are a first-quartile investor, you'll be making only fourth-quartile investment transactions.

Sound harsh? Maybe. But wouldn't more individual investors be hurt more deeply—and more seriously—if they innocently tried the "mission

[5] The very largest institutions each pay Wall Street $1 billion annually and pay their leading stockbrokers $100 million *apiece,* and the stockbrokers earn it by making the best markets and providing the best research services they can deliver.

impossible" of trying to compete against the 100 largest and most active institutions? This inevitably raises the central question: If you can't beat them, why not join them?

Las Vegas is busy every day, so we know not everyone is rational. If you—like Walter Mitty—still fantasize that you can and will beat the pros, you'll need both luck and prayers.

3

MR. MARKET
AND MR. VALUE

THE STOCK MARKET is fascinating *and* very deceptive—in the *short* run. In the very *long* run the market is almost boringly reliable and predictable.

Understanding the personalities of two very different characters is vital to a realistic understanding of the stock market and of yourself as an investor. These very different characters are Mr. Market and Mr. Value.

Mr. Market gets all the attention because he's so interesting, while poor old Mr. Value goes about his important work almost ignored by investors. It's not fair because Mr. Value does all the work while Mr. Market has all the fun *and* causes all the trouble.

Introduced by Benjamin Graham,[1] who also introduced professionalism to investing, Mr. Market lets his enthusiasms *or* his fears run away with him. Emotionally unstable, Mr. Market sometimes feels euphoric and sees only the favorable factors affecting a business and at other times feels so depressed that he can see nothing but trouble ahead. Totally unreliable and quite unpredictable, Mr. Market tries again and again to get us to do something—anything, but at least something. The more activity, the better.

---

[1] In *The Intelligent Investor* (New York, HarperCollins, 1949).

To provoke us to action, he keeps changing his prices—sometimes quite rapidly. This most accommodating fellow stands ready—day after day—to buy if we want to sell or to sell if we want to buy.

Mr. Market is a mischievous but fascinating fellow who persistently teases investors with gimmicks and tricks such as surprising earnings, startling dividend announcements, sudden surges of inflation, inspiring presidential pronouncements, grim reports of commodity prices, announcements of amazing new technologies, ugly bankruptcies, and even threats of war. These events come from his bag of tricks when they are least expected. Just as magicians use clever deceptions to divert our attention, Mr. Market's very short term distractions can trick us and confuse our thinking about investments.

Mr. Market dances before us without a care in the world. And why not? He has no responsibilities at all. As an economic gigolo, he has only one objective: to be "attractive." Meanwhile, Mr. Value, a remarkably stolid and consistent fellow, never shows—and seldom stimulates—any emotion. He lives in the cold, real world where there is nary a thought about perceptions or feelings. He works all day and all night inventing, making, and distributing goods and services. His job is to grind it out on the shop floor, at the warehouse, and in the store, day after day, doing the real work of the economy. His role may not be emotionally exciting, but it sure is important.

Mr. Value always prevails in the long run. Eventually, Mr. Market's antics—like sand castles on the beach—come to naught. In the real world of business, goods and services are produced and distributed in much the same way and in much the same volume when Mr. Market is "up" as they are when he's "down."[2] Long-term investors want to avoid being shaken or distracted by Mr. Market away from their sound long-term policies for achieving favorable long-term results. (Similarly, wise parents of teenagers avoid hearing—or, worse, remembering—too much of what those teenagers say.)

The daily weather is comparably different from the climate. *Weather* is about the short run; *climate* is about the long run—and that makes all the difference. In choosing a climate in which to build a home, we would not be deflected by last week's weather. Similarly, in choosing a long-term investment program, we don't want to be deflected by temporary market conditions.

---

[2]Unless share prices are so very high or low that these market prices matter in takeovers or public offerings.

If you, like Walter Mitty, still fantasize that you can and will beat the pros, you'll need both luck and prayers.

Investors should ignore that rascal, Mr. Market, and his constant jumping around. The daily quotation of the market averages is not any more important to a long-term investor than the daily weather is to a climatologist or to a family deciding where to make its permanent home. Investors who wisely ignore the deceptive tricks of Mr. Market and pay little or no attention to current price changes will look instead at their *real* investments in *real* companies—and to their growing earnings and dividends—and will concentrate on real results over the long term.

Because it's always the surprising short-term events that Mr. Market uses to grab our attention, spark our emotions, and trick us, experienced investors study the details of the stock market's history.[3] The more you study history, the better, because the more you know about how securities markets *have* behaved in the past, the more you'll understand their true nature and how they *will* behave. Such an understanding enables us to live *rationally* with markets that would otherwise seem very *irrational.* At least we would not get shaken loose from our long-term strategy by the short-term tricks and deceptions of Mr. Market's gyrations. Only knowing history and understanding its lessons can insulate us from being surprised. Just as a teenage driver is genuinely amazed by his or her all too predictable accidents—"Dad, the guy came out of *nowhere!*"—investment managers are surprised by adverse performance caused by "anomalies" and "six sigma events." Actually, those surprises are all within life's bell curve of the normal distribution of experience. They are *not* truly "surprises": They are actuarial *expectations.*

Of course, most professional investment managers would have good performance—comfortably better than the market averages—*if* they could eliminate a few "disappointing" investments or a few "difficult" periods in the market. (And most teenagers would have fine driving records if they could expunge a few "surprises.") However, the grim reality of life is that

---

[3] Airline pilots spend hours and hours in flight simulators, "flying" through simulated storms and other unusual crises so that they are accustomed to all sorts of otherwise stressful circumstances and will be well prepared to remain calm and rational when faced with those situations in real life.

most investment managers (and most teenage drivers) are almost certain to experience "anomalous" events. In investing, these anomalous events occur when an unusual (or unanticipated) event or situation—quite unexpected and almost certain never to recur in exactly the same way again—suddenly wipes out what otherwise would have been superior investment performance.[4]

The long term *is* inevitable. It's regression to the mean all over again. That's why "unusually favorable" or high stock prices—as much as you love them—are not good for you. Eventually, you'll have to give back every single increment of return you get that's above the long-term central trend.

Investing is *not* entertainment—it's a responsibility—and investing is not supposed to be "interesting." It's a continuous process, like refining petroleum or manufacturing cookies, chemicals, or integrated circuits. If anything in the process is interesting, it's *wrong*. That's why benign neglect is, for most investors, the secret of long-term success.

The hardest work in investing is not intellectual, it's emotional. Being rational in an emotional environmental is not easy. The hardest work is not figuring out the optimal investment policy; it's sustaining a long-term focus at market highs or market lows and staying committed to sound investment policy. Holding on to sound policy at market highs and market lows is notoriously hard *and* important work, particularly with Mr. Market always trying to trick you into making changes.

In either case, emotions are strongest and current market action appears most demanding of change because the apparent "facts" seem most compelling at market highs—and at market lows.

---

[4]In *The Right Stuff,* Tom Wolfe tells how "unique events" keep causing serious "inexplicable" accidents among test pilots. The young pilots never catch on that these very unusual events are, sadly, an integral part of the dangers inherent in their striving to achieve superior performance.

THE INVESTOR'S DREAM TEAM

WHICH GREAT INVESTORS WOULD YOU INCLUDE in your Investor's Dream Team if you could have anyone—and everyone—you wanted as colleague-investors working with you all day every day?

Warren Buffett? Done deal. He and Charlie Munger are on your team. Peter Lynch? He's yours, *and* all the analysts and fund managers at Fidelity will join you too. John Neff? Got him—*and* all the professionals at Vanguard and Wellington. George Soros? He's on your side too—and so are all the best hedge fund managers across the country. In fact, you can have all the best portfolio managers in the country *and* all the analysts who work for them.

Don't stop there. You can also have all the best analysts on Wall Street—300 at Merrill Lynch, 300 at Goldman Sachs, and 300 at Morgan Stanley—plus nearly equal numbers at Credit Suisse First Boston, Lehman Brothers, and Bear Stearns *and* all the "boutique" analysts specializing in technology or emerging markets.

In fact, you can have *all* the best professionals working for you *all* the time. All you have to do is agree to accept all their best thinking without asking questions.[1] To get the combined expertise of all these top professionals, all you do is *index*—because an index fund replicates the market, and today's professional-dominated stock market reflects all the accumulated expertise of all those diligent experts making their best current judgments. And as they learn more, they are free to change their judgments at any time, and so you will always have the most up-to-date consensus.

Not only do you get the benefits of having the Investor's Dream Team work for you, you get other important benefits automatically. Peace of mind is one. Most individual investors endure regret and anxiety about potential regret. Both are unnecessary. And for those who go with the Investor's Dream Team and index, there are several more powerful competitive advantages: lower fees, lower taxes, and lower "operating" expenses. These persistent costs mount up unrelentingly and do as much harm to investment portfolios as termites do to homes.

The largest part of any portfolio's total long-term returns will come from the simplest investment decision that can be made, and by far the easiest to implement: buying the market.

Hopelessly unpopular with investment managers—and with most clients—the "market portfolio" or index fund is actually the result of all the hard work being done every day by the Investor's Dream Team. Ironically, accepting the consensus of the experts is not popular. The pejoratives range from "settling for average" to "un-American." Passive investing is seldom given anything like the respect it deserves. But it will, over time, achieve better results than will most professional investment managers.

Active investment managers—particularly those with good records—accept the proposition that the market portfolio achieves good long-term returns, but they see an opportunity and challenge to do better. "Even 1 percent on a $100 million or $500 million portfolio is a lot of money—particularly when it's 1 percent compounded year after year—and well worth going after."

They may be right. Some *will* be right. But clients should know that they won't *all* be right. Indeed, the evidence so far is that a great majority of managers will not. Their clients would have done better in a market or index fund.

Considering the time, cost, and effort devoted to achieving better than market results, the index fund certainly produces a lot for a little. This dull

---

[1] Most of us do the same sort of thing every time we fly: assume that our pilots are trained for and committed to safety. Boring as it may seem, we relax in our seats and leave the flying to the experts.

workhorse portfolio may appear virtually mindless but is in fact based on an extensive body of research about markets and investments that is well worth examining and can be summarized briefly.

To summarize, the securities market is an open, free, and competitive market in which large numbers of well-informed and price-sensitive investors and professional investment managers compete skillfully, vigorously, and continuously as both buyers and sellers. Nonexperts can easily retain the services of experts. Prices are quoted widely and promptly. Effective prohibitions against market manipulations are established. And arbitrageurs, traders, hedge funds, market technicians, and longer-term "fundamental" investors seek to find and profit from any market imperfections. Such a market is considered "efficient"—not perfect, and not even perfectly efficient, but sufficiently efficient that wise investors will recognize that they cannot expect to exploit its inefficiencies regularly. In an efficient market, changes in prices follow the pattern described as a "random walk," which means that even close observers of the market—"tape readers"—will not be able to find patterns in securities prices with which to predict future price changes on which they can make profits.

Moreover, because other competing investors are well-informed buyers and sellers, particularly when they are considered in the aggregate, it is unlikely that any one investment manager can regularly obtain profit increments for a large portfolio through fundamental research, because so many other equally dedicated professionals will also be using the best research they can obtain to make their appraisals of whether and when to sell or buy. The more you believe the market is efficient, the more you will believe the rule that the more numerous the skillful competitors are, the less likely it is that anyone will achieve consistently superior results.

In a perfectly efficient market, prices not only reflect any information that could be inferred from the historical sequence of prices but also incorporate and impound all that is knowable[2] about the companies whose stocks are being traded. An efficient market does not mean that stocks will always sell at the "right" price. Investors can be quite *wrong* in their collective judgments—overly optimistic or overly pessimistic—and this will show up in later changes in prices. A market can be quite clumsy on valuations and still be very efficient at incorporating into market prices any available market information and fundamental information about companies. (That's

[2] While there is some specialized evidence that quarterly earnings reports and information on "insider transactions" are not immediately and completely discounted in securities prices, the apparent opportunities to be exploited are so limited that managers of large portfolios would not be able to make effective use of this kind of information anyway.

why the best opportunities for active investment managers to add value may come from being wiser and less susceptible to the psychology of the crowd than others are.)

America's most successful investor, Warren Buffett, recommends that individual investors consider indexing.

An index fund provides investment managers and their clients with an easy alternative. They do not have to play the more complex games of equity investing unless they *want* to play.

This is a marvelous freedom of choice. The option to use an index fund enables any investment manager always to keep pace with the market virtually without effort. It allows you to play only when and where and only for so long as you really want to—and to select any part of the wide investment spectrum for deliberate action at any time for as long or as brief a period as you wish.

For investors, the ability to call "time out" and to invest at any time in an index fund is an important advantage because superior knowledge and skill are not consistent attributes of investment managers. Superior knowledge is a *variable*. This freedom not to play carries the reciprocal responsibility to play only for cause and only when the incremental reward fully justifies the incremental risk.

Even America's most successful investor, Warren Buffett, recommends that individual investors consider indexing. "Let me add a few thoughts about your own investments. Most investors, both institutional and individual, will find that the best way to own common stocks is through an index fund that charges minimal fees. Those following this path are sure to beat the net results (after fees and expenses) delivered by the great majority of investment professionals."[3]

Index funds offer a stunning proposition. Based on the facts of the matter, they offer

- Higher returns
- Lower fees
- Lower operating costs

[3] Berkshire Hathaway, 1996, Annual Report.

- Lower taxes

- Lower risk of errors or blunders

- Lower anxiety about errors or blunders

Active managers can do better, and some will do better some of the time. But *if* certain active managers had been doing significantly better—particularly *after* taxes, fees, expenses, and errors—don't you suppose we'd all know?

Investors would be wise to devote more attention to understanding the real advantages offered by the market fund—the product of the Investor's Dream Team.

5

POGO'S LAMENT

POGO,[1] THAT FAVORITE FOLK PHILOSOPHER, shrewdly observed an essential truth that has particular meaning for investors: "We have met the enemy—and it's us." That is so true.

As "Adam Smith" (George G. W. Goodman) wisely explained, "If you don't know who you really are, the stock market is an expensive place to find out." We are emotional because we are human. We believe that we'll do better when we try harder. We find it hard to take advice such as "If it ain't broke, don't fix it." We are not entirely—or even close to being almost entirely—rational.

Economists traditionally assume that people know what they want to achieve, know how to achieve it, and consistently strive to make rational, unemotional self-interested decisions so that they will achieve their objectives. Behavioral economists[2] show that this is not always how people behave. As people, we are not always rational, and we do not always act in our own best interests. Here's some of what we actually do:

- We ignore the "base rate" or normal pattern of experience. (Even though we *know* the odds are against us, we gamble at casinos.)

[1]Created by the cartoonist Walt Kelly.

[2]Amos Tversky and David Kahnman at Hebrew University in Jerusalem made important discoveries in the late 1960s about how people make "nonrational" decisions concerning their economic interests. Gary Belsky and Thomas Gilovich summarized the lessons of behavioral economics in their book *Why Smart People Make Big Money Mistakes* (New York: Simon and Schuster, 1999).

- We believe in "hot hands" and winning streaks and believe that recent events matter, even in flipping coins.

- We are impressed by short-term success, as in mutual fund perform-ance.

- We are "confirmation-biased," looking for and overweighting the sig-nificance of data that support our initial impressions.

- We allow ourselves to use an initial idea or fact as a reference point for future decisions even when we know it is "just a number."

- We distort our perceptions of our decisions—almost always in our favor—so that we believe we are better than we really are at making decisions. And we don't learn; we stay overconfident.

- We confuse familiarity with knowledge and understanding.

- As investors, we overreact to good news—and to bad news.

- We think we know more relative to others than we really do. (We also think we are "above average" as car drivers, in evaluating other peo-ple, as parents, and as investors. On average, we also believe our children are above average.)

We now know that as human beings we are endowed with certain inalienable characteristics of mind and behavior that compel us to make imperfect decisions—even dreadfully serious mistakes—as investors. For example, we are:

- *Impatient.* If your investments went up 10 percent a year, that would be less than 1 percent a month. On a *daily* basis, that rate of change would be anything but "interesting." (Test yourself: How often do you check the prices of your stocks? If you check more than once a quarter, you are satisfying your curiosity more than your need for price information.)

- *Optimistic.* Being hopeful is almost always helpful, but in investing it's much better to be objective and realistic.

- *Proud.* Over and over again studies show that we substantially over-estimate our own investment performance relative to the market. And we don't like to recognize and acknowledge our mistakes even to ourselves.

- *Emotional.* We smile when our stocks go up and frown or kick the cat when our stocks go down. And our feelings get stronger and stronger the more—and the faster—the prices of our stocks rise or fall.

Our internal demons and enemies are pride, fear, greed, exuberance, and anxiety. These are the "buttons" that Mr. Market wants to push. If you have them, that rascal will find them. No wonder we are such easy prey for Mr. Market with all his attention-getting tricks.

That's why the best way to start learning how to be a successful investor is to follow the standard instruction: know thyself. As an investor, your capabilities in two major realms will determine most of your success: your intellectual capabilities and your emotional capabilities.

Your *intellectual* capabilities include your skills in analyzing financial statements (balance sheets, funds flow accounts, and income statements), the extent and accuracy of your ability to store and recall information, how extensively you can correlate and integrate various bits of data and information into insight and understanding, how much knowledge you can master and manage, and the like.

Your *emotional* capabilities include your ability to be calm and rational despite the chaos and disruptions that will—thanks to Mr. Market—intrude abruptly upon you and your decision making.

Each investor has a zone of competence (the kind of investing for which she or he has real skill) and a zone of confidence (the area of investing in which she or he will be calm and comfortable). Where your spheres overlap in a Venn diagram is where you should always take up a position. (In the trade-off between the conflicting investor goals of "eat well" and "sleep well," the sage advice is to "sell down to the sleeping point." Don't go outside your zone of confidence because outside that zone you may get emotional, and being emotional is never good for your investing.

FIGURE 5-1 Venn diagram.

If you know yourself—your strengths *and* weaknesses—you will know the limits you must learn to live within each realm: your zone of comfort and your zone of competence. Where these zones overlap—in a Venn diagram—is your investor's sweet spot (see Figure 5-1). That's where you want to concentrate: where you have the right skills *and* the right temperment to do your best investing.

Know your strengths *and* your limits because a strong defense is the best foundation for a strong offense. Stay inside your comfort and competence zones. After all, it *is* your money, so treat it with the care and respect it deserves, investing only when you know from experience that you have the requisite competence *and* can be consistently rational.

C H A P T E R

6

YOUR UNFAIR COMPETITIVE ADVANTAGE

ALL GREAT STRATEGISTS SEEK to establish a sustainable advantage over their competitors:

- That's why army generals want to "take the high ground" and have the advantage of surprise.

- That's why coaches want stronger, taller, faster players; strive for even better conditioning; and care a lot about team spirit and motivation.

- That's why corporate strategists attempt to create "branding" franchises for their products and services and try to establish loyalty among each group of customers.

- That's why corporations strive to move up the "experience curve"— so that their unit costs of manufacture will be lower than any competitor's. Patent protection, Food and Drug Administration approval, low-cost transportation, technological leadership, consumer preferences, and trademarks all have one thing in common: competitive advantage.

37

In each case strategists are trying to identify and obtain a significant and sustainable strategic advantage—what competitors will ultimately complain is an "unfair" competitive advantage. In investing, there are four ways to achieve an "unfair" competitive advantage and beat the market.

The *physically* difficult way to "beat the market" is the most popular, or at least the most widely used. Believers get up earlier in the morning and stay up later at night and work on weekends. They carry heavier briefcases and read more reports, make and take more phone calls, and go to more meetings. They strive physically to do more and work faster so that they can get ahead of the market.

The *intellectually* difficult approach to beating the market is used by only a few investors, including a few whose skills inspire us all. They strive to think more deeply and farther into the future so that they can gain truly superior insight and understanding of particular investment opportunities.

The *emotionally* difficult approach to superior investing is to maintain calm rationality at all times, never get excited by favorable market events, and never get upset by market events or adverse markets.

The fourth way to achieve superior results is the easiest way. But who among us actually finds it easy to pay no attention and sustain that most useful stance: benign neglect? That's where personal modesty comes into play and is very much needed. You are well suited to the "easy" way if you can examine the facts of the situation and accept the conclusion that your own efforts are unlikely to improve on a passive acceptance of reality, as we all do with weather conditions and when flying long distances as passengers—and as more investors are learning is wise when investing in today's highly professionalized markets. The *easy* way to gain—and sustain—an unfair competitive advantage as an investor is to invest through index funds.

Here are the "unfair" advantages of index investing in today's market environment:

- Higher rates of return, because over the long term, 85 percent of active managers fall short of the market.

- Lower management fees: 15 to 20 basis points versus 50 to 60 point fees every year.

- Lower operating expenses: 5 basis points versus 50 to 75 basis points.

- Lower commissions because portfolio turnover is a lot less: under 10 percent.

- Lower "market impact" because portfolio turnover is a lot less: under 10 percent.

- Lower taxes. Fewer profits are "recognized" each year—particularly as short-term profits—because turnover is lower.

- Freedom from error or blunder because no market timing or portfolio strategy decisions are required *and* because no single stock ever represents a dominant position in the portfolio.

- Less anxiety or concern because you never have to worry that you might be making mistakes of omission or commission that will result in unusual losses or missed opportunities.

Warren Buffett estimates[1] what he considers the annual "horrendous costs" of contemporary active investing to be:

- Over $40 billion—on just the shares of Fortune 500 companies—for executing transactions at 6 cents per share.

- $35 billion for management fees, expenses, sales load, wrap fees, and so on.

- $25 billion for a miscellany of spreads on futures and options, costs of variable annuities, and the like.

Noting that this is "just" 1 percent of the total market value of the Fortune 500, Buffett—always seeing reality as an *owner* should—reminds us that this $100 billion cuts a big chunk out of the $334 billion the whole Fortune 500 earned in 1998 so that investors are earning less than $250 billion—just 2½ percent—on their investment of $10 *trillion*. That 2½ percent return on investment is, in his view, "slim pickings."

Another "leak" in an investor's return comes with taxes driven by portfolio turnover. The more turnover, the more taxes *and* the lower the accumulated returns. (With short-term gains, which are so often realized in mutual funds, the negative impact of taxes is even greater.) The impact of turnover—and of taxes on turnover—is shown starkly in Figure 6-1.

Each index fund replicates a particular index of the stock market. However, although each index is designed to replicate the market or a sector of the market fairly and accurately, indexes are not all created equal. They differ. Usually the differences are small and inconsequential, but in some markets, differences between indexes—and the index funds that track them—are sig-

[1]*Fortune,* November 22, 1999.

FIGURE 6-1 $1,000,000 initial investment compounded at a 15% pretax annual rate of return over a 20-year period, assuming a 27% tax rate on all realized gains.

Pretax Rate of Return	Annual Turnover	Value of $1,000,000 Initial Investment at the End of 20 Years	After-Tax Rate of Return
15%	0	$16,366,500	15.5%
15	3%	14,780,800	14.4
15	10	12,386,300	13.4
15	30	9,694,000	12.0
15	85	8,136,600	11.1
15	100	7,990,800	10.95

nificant. For example, in 2000 the S&P 500 had heavy weightings in several very "large-cap" stocks selling at very high—presumably unsustainable—price/earnings multiples during the Internet euphoria. Predictably, these high flyers returned to earth, bringing down the S&P 500—and equally bringing down the index funds that accurately matched the S&P 500.

Investors had three sensible choices. One choice was a patient "this too shall pass" attitude. The second choice was to invest in a broader "total market" index fund. The third choice was to be somewhat "contrarian" and invest in an index fund matched to a major area of the stock market that was currently not popular, such as low P/E "value" stocks. For most investors the middle way—a "total market" index fund—is the most sensible.

C H A P T E R

7

THE PARADOX

A PARADOX IS HAUNTING investment management.

The paradox is that funds with very long-term purposes are being managed to meet short-term objectives that may be neither feasible nor important. And these funds are *not* being managed to achieve long-term objectives that are both feasible and worthwhile.

The unimportant and difficult task to which most investment managers devote most of their time with little or no success is trying to "beat the market." Realistically—without taking above-average market risk—outperforming the equity market by even one-half of 1 percent *consistently* would be a great success which almost no sizable investment managers have achieved for very long.

The truly important but not very difficult task to which investment managers and their clients could and should devote themselves involves four steps: (1) understanding the client's real needs, (2) defining realistic investment objectives that can meet the client's realistic needs, (3) establishing the right asset mix for each portfolio, and (4) developing well-reasoned, sensible investment policies designed to achieve the client's realistic and specified long-term investment objectives. In this work, success can be achieved easily.

For example, if the long-term average rate of return on bonds is 6 percent and the return from investments in common stocks is 10 percent—because there must be a higher long-term rate of return on stocks to persuade investors to accept the risk of equity investing—shifting just 10 percent of the portfolio's assets from bonds to stocks and keeping it there would over time increase the portfolio's average annual rate of return by $\frac{4}{10}$ of 1 percent (4 percent higher return on stocks × 10 percent of assets = 0.40 percent).

Shifting the asset mix of a 60 percent equity/40 percent fixed-income portfolio to 70:30 may not be a major proposition, but as was noted in an earlier chapter, consistently beating the market rate of return by 0.4 percentage points (or 40 basis points) a year through superior stock selection would be a substantial achievement.

The problem is not in the market but in ourselves.

Very few professional investors have been able to sustain such superior results. It is ironic that a change of even such modest magnitude in the basic asset allocation decision can result in an improvement in total return significantly greater than the elusive increment sought in the beat-the-market syndrome.

Clearly, if the asset mix truly appropriate to the client's objectives required an even more substantial emphasis on equities—such as 80:20, 90:10, or even 100:0—the incremental rate of return over the 60:40 portfolio will be even greater: 0.8 percent annually at 80:20 and 1.6 percent average annually at 100 percent. Virtually no large investment manager can hope to beat the market by such magnitudes.

Of course, these calculations are mechanical. They present averages, ignoring the fact that actual returns in individual years come in an impressive and even alarming distribution of actual annual returns around these averages.

The crucial question is not simply whether long-term returns on common stocks would exceed returns on bonds or bills *if* the investor held on through the many startling gyrations of the market. The crucial question is whether the investor will in fact hold on for the long term so that the expected average returns will be achieved. The problem is not in the market but in ourselves, our perceptions, and our reactions to our perceptions.

During the 15 years from 1982 to 1997 mutual funds averaged approximately 15 percent in annual returns. However, mutual fund *investors* averaged only 10 percent. Why? Because instead of developing an astute long-term investing program and staying with it, investors jumped around from one fund to another. The result was the loss of a full one-third of the total returns earned by their funds—but *not* earned for themselves. This is why it is so important for you to develop a realistic understanding of investing and of capital markets and to develop a realistic knowledge of your own tolerance for market fluctuations and your long-term investment objectives or, if you are serving on an investment committee for a corporate pension fund or a college's endowment, for that organization's tolerance for market fluctuations. The more you know about yourself as an investor and the more you understand the securities markets, the more you will know what long-term asset mix is really right for your portfolios and the more likely it is that you will be able to sustain your commitment for the long term.

For investors, the real opportunity to achieve superior results lies not in scrambling to outperform the market but in establishing *and adhering to* appropriate investment policies over the long term—policies that position the portfolio to benefit from riding with the main long-term forces in the market. An investment policy that is wisely formulated by realistic and well-informed clients with a long-term perspective and clearly defined objectives is the foundation on which portfolios should be constructed and managed over time and through market cycles.

In reality, very few investors have developed such investment policies. And because they have not, most investment managers are left to manage their clients' portfolios without knowing their clients' real objectives and without the discipline of explicit agreement on their mission as investment managers. *This is the client's fault.*

Investment policy is the foundation on which portfolios should be constructed and managed.

As a result of not knowing enough about the particular facts and values of their different clients, investment managers typically manage all funds in virtually the same way and with very nearly the same asset mix, even in extraordinarily different kinds of funds.

The problem of a procrustean "one size fits all" asset mix is even more worrisome when the clients are individuals. While most investment managers would in theory like to match the portfolios they manage to the specific needs and objectives of each client, the reality is that most managers work with a small number of standard asset mixes and assign clients to those few alternatives. While the professionalism of investment counseling is more profound than the professionalism of managing investment portfolios—and can make far more of an economic difference to the client over the long term—most clients will neither do the disciplined work of formulating sound long-term investment policies for themselves nor pay sufficient fees to make counseling adequately rewarding for investment managers to provide this much more important service.

The sobering conclusion from experience is that while investment policy conforming to the client's particular investment objectives may be honored in theory, it is little used in practice. Getting it right on investment policy is up to you the investor. After all, it's your money.

The differences among employee benefit plans can be substantial, but these differences will matter only if the special characteristics of their company or institution's investment goals are being determined when basic investment policies are being formulated or reviewed.

It is hardly conceivable that senior corporate management would routinely delegate full operating responsibility for comparable millions of dollars[1] to regular operating divisional executives—let alone a manager not directly supervised by top management—with only broad guidelines or instructions such as: "Try to do better than average" or "You're the experts; see what you can do for us."

College trustees know the most about the linkages between the endowment and the annual budget or fund-raising. Corporate executives will know their pension plan's actuarial assumptions and how close to reality those assumptions really are; the company's tolerance for intrusions on its quarter-to-quarter and year-to-year progression of reported earnings by a sudden need to fund a deficit in plan assets caused by an abrupt drop in their market value; the company's evolving philosophy of employee benefits and how benefit programs might be changed; the company's likelihood of increasing benefits to retired plan participants to protect their purchasing power from the corrosion of inflation; the tolerance for interim market fluctuations among staff, senior executives, and the board of directors; each corporations's obligations—formal and informal—to its employees; its capital structure; and its sensitivity to unexpected calls for funding past

---

[1]At some companies, pension fund assets are larger than the sponsoring corporation's net worth. For wealthy families, astute management of their existing portfolio of investments is clearly the most important dimension of their financial futures.

service obligations. The "risk tolerance" of a corporate pension plan sponsor is not just the risk tolerance of the pension staff or even the senior financial officer; it is the risk tolerance of a majority of the board of directors at the moment of most severe market adversity. At endowments, it's the risk tolerance of a majority of the board of trustees. In either case, it is not the rational behavior expected during a normal market; it's the behavior that may be driven by real worries during market extremes.

The same is just as true—and always will be just as true—for individual investors. Know what you really want and make it happen. Only you will know enough to speak with relevance and credibility to such important characteristics as the amount, timing, and certainty of flows *out* of the fund. Only the client knows her own (or her organization's) tolerance for changes in market prices—particularly at market extremes where it really matters—because it is at such stress periods that investment policies seem least certain and the pressure for change is most strong.

You know the most about your overall financial and investment situation—your earning power, your ability to save, your obligations for children's educational expenses, or the likely timing and scale of needs for spendable funds or how you feel about investments.

The real question is not whether portfolio managers are constructing portfolios to match the goals and objectives of each specific client. (The uninspiring reality is that they do not.) The relevant question is: Who is responsible for bringing about the requisite change? The pragmatic answer is that the responsibility is not going to be fulfilled by investment managers. It will be left up to the client. You can and should accept this responsibility.

You can do more for your portfolio's long-term rate of return by developing and sustaining wise long-range policies that commit you to an appropriate structure of investments than can be done by the most skillful manipulation of the individual holdings within the portfolio.

In brief, you should recognize that portfolio operations are subordinate to investment policy, and you should assert your responsibility for leadership in policy formation. This is not an investment problem that should be left to portfolio managers—no matter how skilled and conscientious they are—any more than, as Clemenceau cautioned, war should be left to the generals. It is your problem, and while responsibility for it can be abdicated, it really cannot be delegated.

Here are six important questions each client should think through and then explain his answers to his own investment manager. (Investment managers would be wise to urge their clients to do this kind of "homework.")

First, what are the real risks of an adverse outcome, particularly in the short run? Unacceptable risks should never be taken. For example, it would not make sense to invest all of a high school senior's college tuition savings in the stock market because if the market went down, the student might not be able to pay the tuition bill. Nor would it make sense to invest money saved for a house in stocks just two or three years before the intended date of purchase.

Second, what are the probable emotional reactions of clients to an adverse experience? As the axiom goes, some investors care about *eating* well and some care about *sleeping* well. You should know and stay well within your tolerance—hopefully, a well-informed tolerance—for interim fluctuations in portfolio value. The emphasis on *informed tolerance* is deliberate. Avoidance of market risk does have a real "opportunity cost," and the client should be fully informed of the sorts of interim gains and losses that should be anticipated with each incremental level of market risk taken—and the opportunity cost of each level of market risk *not* taken.

Third, how knowledgeable are you about investments and the vagaries of financial markets? Investing does not always "make sense" to the non-professional. Sometimes it seems almost perversely counterintuitive. Lack of knowledge tends to make investors too cautious in bear markets and too confident in bull markets—sometimes at a considerable cost.

Managers should be careful *not* to assume that their clients are more sophisticated than they really are. Portfolio managers can help their clients by explaining the way capital markets behave—and misbehave—and clients can help educate themselves about the differences between short-term experiences and long-term experiences.

A client who is very well informed about the investment environment will know what to expect. This client will be able to take in stride the disruptive experiences that may cause other, less informed investors to overreact to either unusually favorable or unusually adverse market experiences.

Fourth, what other capital or income resources does the client have, and how important is the particular portfolio to the client's *overall* financial position? For example, pension funds sponsored by large and prosperous corporations can reasonably accept greater market risk than can a college endowment, which may have difficulty raising capital to replenish losses. A young business executive with a generous pension fund for safety can take greater short-term market risks in his personal investments. A retired widow usually cannot accept as much risk as can her alma mater.

Fifth, are there any legal restrictions on investment policy? Many personal trust funds are quite specific. Many endowment funds have restrictions that can be significant, particularly when they specify how income is to be defined or spent or both.[2]

Sixth, are there any unanticipated consequences of interim fluctuations in portfolio value that might affect policy? A frequently cited example is the risk in a pension fund of being obliged to augment contributions if the portfolio's market value drops below a "trigger" level built into the actuaries' calculations of current contributions. Universities would be reluctant to abort educational and research programs to which the faculty members were committed. Alumni giving might be affected by perceptions of endowment management. And we all know that it can be very hard for individual investors to continue taking the very long-term view when markets are rising rapidly—or, worse, falling rapidly.

Each of these possible concerns should be examined rigorously to ascertain how much deviation from the normally optimal investment policy—broad diversification at a moderately above-average market risk—is truly warranted. Understanding and using these insights in the specific realities of the particular client's situation and objectives is the basis on which wise investment policies should be developed for each different portfolio.

In pursuing the goal of developing and using wise investment policies, we must first recognize that most *institutional* funds such as pensions and endowments are *un*owned money: They do not really "belong" to anyone. There is no individual who can or would say, "This is my money. *This* is what I want you to do with it. Or else." There are, in other words, no principals.

On the other hand, with individual funds, the investor is the principal—and all too often is the "principal problem" because he or she wants to do something. Unfortunately, for the activist investor, history teaches that in investing patience and fortitude—or benign neglect—are more beneficial than activity. To rephrase the familiar admonition: "Don't just do something, stand there!"

Second, we should recognize that those who are nominally "at the controls" at most institutional funds are usually only midlevel representatives of an organization and are subject to after-the-fact criticism by powerful Monday-morning quarterbacks. These representatives have clear economic incentives to protect their careers: "It may not be my money, but it *is* my job and my career."

---

[2]As William Carey and Craig Bright advocate in *The Law and the Lore of Endowment Funds* (1969), restrictions should be carefully examined because they may not in fact be as confining as they may initially appear.

The careers of these institutional representatives seldom hinge on the work they do in setting investment policy or managing investment managers, but "career torpedoes" can come with 20-20 hindsight.

In such circumstances, what pattern of behavior would we expect from these representatives? Naturally, they will be self-protective and defensive and will make their decisions with reference to a relatively short time period, say, three to five years. They will not seek to optimize; they will seek the most acceptable near-term balance between desires for superior returns and avoidance of unusual or unorthodox positions. Above all, they will avoid any unnecessarily distressing risk to their own careers!

Investors must assert their role as experts on their own needs.

What are most investment managers doing? The very same thing. While they may be bold when they and their firms are young and just getting started, once they get established, they want to keep their accounts. They are understandably cautious, even too cautious. They are compromising with an overly defensive tilt: hugging the index and worrying too much about not losing the accounts they manage.

Observers of the paradox that haunts investment management say it is unrealistic to expect investment managers to risk strained client relationships by insisting on a well-conceived and carefully articulated investment policy with explicit objectives when their clients seem uninterested in going through the discipline.

Escape from the paradox depends on clients asserting their role as experts on their own needs and resources and insisting on appropriate investment goals and policies.

For that, we must look not to the agents but to the principals. However, in institutional investment management there *are* no principals. And all too few individual investors will assert themselves, assuming that the professionals know more or know better. If investors are not willing to act like principals, we can be sure that the paradox will remain for a long time. In this case, individual investors have an important opportunity to outperform institutional investors by designing and deliberately achieving the optimal match between their real investment objectives and the long-term investment policy that's best for each of them.

While you cannot beat the market, you can exploit the fact that so many others are trying to do so. That's why the Investor's Dream Team creates such an unusually attractive—high value and low cost—alternative approach: indexing.

By "looking the other way," you can focus on what really matters: not the futile struggle to beat the market but the reasoned and highly achievable goal of setting, and meeting, your own long-term investment objectives. The more clearly you recognize that others are paying attention to the wrong thing, the more calmly and firmly you can pay attention to the right thing.

8

TIME

TIME IS ARCHIMEDES' LEVER in investing.

Archimedes is often quoted as saying, "Give me a lever long enough and a place to stand, and I can move the earth." In investing, that lever is *time* (and the place to stand, of course, is on a firm and realistic investment policy).

Time—the length of time investments will be held, the period of time over which investment results will be measured and judged—is the single most powerful factor in any investment program.

If time is *short,* the highest-return investments—the ones a long-term investor naturally most wants to own—will be undesirable, and a wise short-term investor will avoid them. But if the time period for investing is abundantly *long,* a wise investor can commit without great anxiety to investments that appear to be very risky in the short run.

Given enough time, investments that might otherwise seem unattractive may become highly desirable. Time transforms investments from *least* attractive to *most* attractive—and vice versa—because while the average expected rate of return is not at all affected by time, the range or distribution of *actual* returns around the expected average is very greatly affected. The longer the time period over which investments are held, the closer the actual returns in a *portfolio*[1] will come to the expected average.

---

[1] The actual returns on *individual* investments, in contrast, will be more and more widely dispersed as the time period lengthens.

As a result, time changes the ways in which different kinds of investments can best be used by different investors with different situations and
objectives.

The conventional time period over which rates of return are calculated—their average *and* their distribution—is one year. While convenient
and widely used, this 12-month time frame simply does not match the time
available to all the different kinds of investors with all their different constraints and purposes. For example, some investors are investing for only a
few days at a time, while others will hold their investments for several
decades. It is the difference in time horizon that really matters.

To show how important time is, let's exaggerate for effect and look at
the returns expected in a *one-day* investment in common stocks.

Short-term risk should not be a major concern to long-term investors.

The typical stock's share price is $40, and the range of trading during
the day might easily be from 39¼ to 40½—a range of 1¼, or 3.1 percent of
the average price for the day. Remembering that in today's market—with
today's expectations for future inflation—the average annual rate of return
for common stocks in recent years has been approximately 15 percent, let's
postulate that an investment in this hypothetical stock would have an
expected daily return of 0.06 percent (15 percent annual return divided by
250 trading days) and a range around that expected average of plus or
minus 1.55 percent (3.1 percent intraday range divided by two).

Let's "annualize" that daily return of 0.06 percent and that 3.1 percent
daily variation. The average annual expected rate of return would be 15 percent, but the *range* of returns around the 15 percent would be a daunting
±387.5 percent! (In other words, the annualized rate of return for a one-day
investment in our hypothetical stock would be somewhere between a *profit*
of 405.5 percent and a *loss* of 372.5 percent.)

Of course, no sensible investor would knowingly invest in common
stocks only for a single day or month or even for a year. Such brief time
periods are clearly too short for investments in common stocks because the
expectable *variation* in return is too large in comparison to the average
expected return. The extra uncertainty incurred when investing in common
stocks is not balanced in the very short run by a sufficiently large or sufficiently sure reward. Such short-term holdings in common stocks are not
investments: They are rank speculations.

However, this deliberate one-day burlesque of the conventional use of annual rates of return leads to a serious examination of the differences in investor satisfaction when the measurement period is changed. That examination shows why an investor with a very *long* time horizon might invest entirely in common stocks just as wisely as another investor with a very *short* time horizon would invest only in Treasury bills or a money market fund. The examination also shows why an intermediate-term investor would, as her time horizon is extended outward, shift investment emphasis from money market instruments toward bonds and then more and more toward equities.

Time transforms certain investments from *least* attractive to *most* attractive—and vice versa.

Despite the constancy of the average *expected* rate of return—no matter what the time period is—the profound impact of time on the actual realized rate of return is clearly demonstrated in the charts in Figure 8-1.

FIGURE 8-1 Range of returns of stocks, bonds, and cash, after adjusting for inflation (1900–2000).

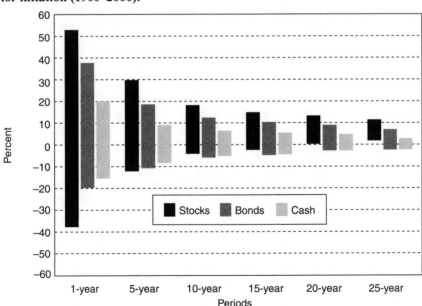

The one-year-at-a-time rates of return on common stocks over the years are almost incoherent. They show both large and small gains and large and small losses occurring in what appears to be a random pattern. At best, you could have earned 53.4 percent in a year, but at worst you could have lost 37.3 percent. It seems absurd to "summarize" those wildly disparate one-year experiences as having any "average" rate of return.

Shifting to five-year periods brings a considerable increase in coherence or regularity. There are, for example, *few* periods with losses, and the periods with gains appear far more *often* and consistently. The reason for this is that as the measurement period lengthens, the average rate of return begins to overpower the single-year differences.

Shifting to 10-year periods increases the consistency of returns significantly. Only *one* loss is experienced, and most periods show average annual gains of 5 to 15 percent. Again, the power of the average rate of return—now compounded over a decade—overwhelms the single-year differences.

Moving on to 20-year periods brings even more consistency to the experienced rate of return. There are no losses, only gains. And the gains cluster more closely together around the long-term expected average rate of return.

Despite the obviously substantial differences in the range or distribution of returns in each time frame, there is one central constant: The *average* actual rate of return is almost the same in all cases. This is the case because the data shown are all samples from the same continuous stream of investment experience.

Appreciating the fact that actual experiences in investing are samples drawn from a continuous stream of experience is vital to understanding the meaning contained in the data. Even in New England, the weather—when considered over a long period of time—becomes a sensible, reliable *climate* even though the days of bitter cold or sweltering heat seem individually so unpredictable, particularly in regard to the exact date of occurrence. Similarly, in investing, the patient observer can see the true underlying patterns that make the seemingly random year-by-year, month-by-month, or day-by-day experiences not disconcerting or confusing but splendidly predictable—on average and over time.

In weather and investments, larger and more numerous samples enable us to come closer and closer to understanding the normal experience from which the sample is drawn. It is this understanding of the normal experience that enables you to design your own behavior so that you can take advantage of the dominant normal pattern over the long term and not be thrown off by the confusing daily events that present themselves with such force in the short term.

The single most important dimension of your investment policy is the asset mix, particularly the ratio of fixed-income investments to equity investments.

Discussions of the asset mix have attracted considerable attention in recent years. Analyses show over and over again that the trade-off between risk and reward is driven by one key factor: time.

Unfortunately, in most cases the time horizon being used is not chosen for the specific fund but is instead a conventional five years. A five-year "horizon" usually leads to the familiar 60:40 ratio of equities to debt. A 10-year horizon leads to an 80:20 ratio. A 15-year horizon typically results in a 90:10 ratio. And so it goes. The unfortunate reality is that none of these time horizons is "right" for a pension fund or a university endowment or even for most individual investors who want to provide financial security for their children. They are all far too short for an investor with an investment horizon of 30 to 50 years or even more.

What is most disturbing about asset mix decisions is not that they are made with an inappropriately short time horizon but that there is almost no evidence that such decisions are made deliberately and explicitly. For example, while their nearly perpetual character enables pension funds to accept interim market risk better than any other type of investor can, the typical pension fund was, in the 1970s, 1980s, and 1990s, only 50 percent in equities. In other words, the time horizon actually being used in managing the typical pension fund was not 30 years or 50 years but only 3 or 4 years.

These funds paid an opportunity cost in returns forgone. As it turned out, the cost of not being fully invested in stocks in the 1980s and 1990s was *very* large: Equities produced record returns, over 15 percent *compounded.*

Investment history documents conclusively (as seen in Chapter 2) that the very first weeks of a market recovery produce a substantial proportion of the gains that will be experienced. Yet it is at the crucial market bottom that a market timer is most likely to be out of the market—missing the very best part. But that is not the point at issue here. The point is that investors should have taken such a cautious asset mix decision only after examining the inherent risks and rewards and deciding what policy would be best for them. Such powerful decisions should be made deliberately and only after a careful examination of long-term realities.

It is clear that if more investors insisted on long-range policy reviews, their funds typically would be invested differently and would earn higher returns.

C H A P T E R

9

RETURNS

I
NVESTMENT RETURNS COME, as everyone knows, in two very different forms: quite predictable cash received from interest or dividends
and gains or losses in market price that are, particularly in the short
run, quite *un*predictable. Investors devote most of their time and
skill trying to increase returns by capitalizing on changes in market
prices—by outsmarting each other. They are making a big mistake.

Changes in market price are caused by changes in the consensus of
active investors about what the price of a stock ought to be. This consensus
is determined by thousands and thousands of institutions and individuals
constantly seeking opportunities for investment profit. To find these opportunities, investors study monetary and fiscal economics and political developments in all the major nations; visit hundreds and hundreds of companies;
attend thousands of breakfast, lunch, and dinner meetings with corporate
executives, economists, industry experts, securities analysts, and other
experts; study reports and analyses produced by hundreds of companies
and dozens of large brokerage firms; read extensively in the industry and
trade press; and talk almost constantly on the telephone with people who
have ideas, information, or insights with which these active investors might
improve their investment performance.

In addition to studying the *rational* world, investors study the irrational
world of "investor psychology," public confidence, politics, and "market
tone," because in the short run the markets—and market prices—are very
human or nonrational. The ways in which investors perceive and interpret
information and the ways they react to developments have a great impact
on market prices, particularly in the short run. Therefore, active investors

are always looking for opportunities to capitalize on changes in other investors' opinions before changes in their own opinions are capitalized on by other investors. Not all of the investors' interpretations and perceptions are "correct." Many, particularly in retrospect, seem very wrong.

Investment management in today's dynamic markets is a wonderful, turbulent, fascinating, hopeful, anguishing, stressful, and euphoric process of competing in the world's most free and competitive market against many talented and ambitious competitors for advantage gained from greater knowledge, wiser interpretation, and better timing. (The irony is that for most investment managers and their clients most of this activity really does not matter—not because these investment managers are not talented but because so many of the managers' competitors are *equally* talented.)

For all the surface complexity in the process, two main areas are dominant in the evaluation of common stocks. The first is the consensus of investors on the probable amount and timing of future earnings and dividends. The second is the consensus of investors on the discount rate at which this stream of estimated future dividends and earnings should be capitalized to establish its present value.

The consensus estimates of future dividends and earnings will vary among different investors and at different times as a result of changes in expectations for secular growth and cyclical fluctuations in unit demand, prices and taxes, discoveries and inventions, changes in the competition at home and abroad, and so forth. Over time, the discount rate considered appropriate will vary with many factors, among which the most important are the perceived risk of the particular investment or investments of its general type, the expected rate of inflation, and the discount factor that converts a stream of expected future payments in dividends or interest into present capital value. But as everyone knows, price and value are not the same thing.

It's not how good you are that counts but how good you are compared with your competitors.

The longer the future period over which estimates—both of earnings and dividends and of the discount rate—must be extended, the greater the day-to-day or month-to-month fluctuations in the stock price that will be caused by changes in the investors' consensus about present value.

Long-term investors understand from experience the remarkable discipline of the bell curve of economic behavior—the normal distribution of events within limiting constraints—and the strong tendency of major forces in the economy and the stock market to move toward "normal." Long-term investors understand that the farther current events are away from the mean at the center of the bell curve, the stronger the forces of mean reversion[1] are, pulling the current data toward the center and "normal." (The more today's temperature is very hot, the more certain it is that tomorrow's temperature will be *less* hot.)

Investors want to know what the most probable investment outlook for the years ahead is. One simple way to look ahead is to appraise the likely *change* in two powerful variables: long-term interest rates and corporate profits. A good way to be realistic is to assume that the future range of interest rates and profits will be within the historical upper and lower limits and will tend toward their respective means. (Caution: If the market has been going up, investors—who usually evaluate future prospects by looking into the *rear*view mirror—will add some upward momentum, and if the market has been trending down, they will add some downward momentum.)

Warren Buffett used this straightforward approach[2] in 1999—when the consensus of experienced investors was that they expected nearly 13 percent annual average returns for the next 10 years—to show why he expected just 6 percent *minus* 2 percent to offset inflation to arrive at estimated *real* returns of 4 percent annually. (Note that the consensus that matters is not today's consensus about the distant future but the consensus that will prevail when we are actually in that distant future.)

The average long-term experience in investing is *never* surprising, but the short-term experience is *always* surprising.

As the time horizon over which an estimate extends is lengthened, the impact of the estimated discount rate becomes more and more dominant (relative to estimates of future earnings and dividends) in regard to the current market price of a security.

---

[1] Sailors know the remarkable power of the "righting arm" as the keel weight puts increasing weight force into making the hull upright as the boat heels farther and farther over. While a landlubber may get more and more anxious about "tipping over," an experienced sailor knows that the forces that prevent further heeling are *increasing*.

[2] *Fortune,* November 1999.

For investment value, by contrast, as the holding period over which an investor owns an investment lengthens, the importance of the discount factor decreases and the importance of the dividends paid increases.

For a very long-term *investor* who cares about value, the relative importance of earnings and dividends received is overwhelming. For a very short-term *speculator* who cares about price, everything depends on the day-to-day and month-to-month changes in investor psychology (or, in more formal terms, the appropriate discount rate) and what people are willing to pay. Like the weather, the average long-term experience in investing is never surprising, but the short-term experience is *always* surprising.

The history of returns on investment, as documented in study after study, shows three basic characteristics:

1. Common stocks have average returns higher than do bonds. Bonds in turn have higher returns than do short-term money market instruments.

2. The daily, monthly, and yearly fluctuations in actual returns on common stocks exceed the fluctuations in returns on bonds, which in turn exceed the fluctuations in returns on short-term money market instruments.

3. The magnitude of the period-to-period fluctuation in rate of return increases as the measurement period is shortened and decreases as the measurement period is lengthened. In other words, rates of return appear more normal over long periods of time.

The really impressive characteristic of investment returns is that the *variation* in year-to-year rates of return on common stocks dwarfs the average annual rate of return on stocks.

We now know that it is nearly nonsense to say, "Common stocks have produced an average rate of return of 9 percent." This is an incomplete and misleading statement. Far better, we could say, "Over the past 50 years, the actual returns have been between a *loss* of 43 percent[3] and a *gain* of 54 percent. While the geometric mean rate of return is about 9 percent, the standard deviation of actual returns around that mean is nearly 22 percent. Finally, we regret to say we cannot give you the sequence with which those returns will be experienced. They, of course, occur at random."

The two statements are remarkably different from each other, particularly for an investor who is suddenly and unexpectedly experiencing the

[3] These rates of return are nominal (preinflation), while the data cited on page 64 are "real" (after being corrected for inflation).

most dreadfully negative year in what was so serenely described as the "normal" bell-shaped distribution. That's why institutional investors and investment managers are learning to describe investment returns in formal statistical terms. Individual investors would be well advised to learn enough about the language of statistics to have an awareness of what is meant by *mean* and *bell curve* or *normal distribution* and what is meant by *two standard deviations* as a measure of the frequency with which unusual events *are* expected and *do* occur.

In addition to learning the importance of describing the distribution of returns around that mean, we have learned to separate out the different components in the average rate of return and analyze each component separately.

There are three main components in the average rate of return:

1.   The *real* risk-free rate of return[4]
2.   A premium over the risk-free rate of return to offset the expected erosion of purchasing power caused by inflation
3.   A premium over the inflation-adjusted risk-free rate of return to compensate investors for accepting market risk

Dividing total returns into these three classes of return makes it possible to compare the returns of each type of investment—stocks, bonds, and bills. This work has been done in a series of landmark studies by Roger Ibbotson and Rex Sinquefield, and the accompanying table from their book shows their major findings for the 55-year period 1926–1991 (see Figure 9-1). The analysis is very informative.[5]

Treasury bills appear to be quite safe and reliable—in nominal terms, not adjusted for inflation—with apparently positive returns in 54 of 55 years. However, when adjusted for inflation, returns are positive just under 60 percent of the time. Even more startling, the average annual rate of return on Treasury bills, after adjusting for inflation, is zero.

In other words, Treasury bills are usually no more than a match for inflation. Most of the time you do get your money back—with its purchasing power intact. But that is all you get. There is virtually no real return *on* your money, just the return *of* your money.

---

[4] There is no risk of default in a Treasury bill because if the government were short of money, it would simply print more.

[5] Roger G. Ibbotson and Rex A. Sinquefield, *Stocks, Bonds, Bills, and Inflation: The Past and the Future* (Charlottesville, VA: Financial Analysts Research Foundation, 1982).

**FIGURE 9-1   Wealth indexes of investments in the U.S. capital markets,
1925–1990 (year end 1925 = 1.00).**

*Source: Stocks, Bonds, Bills, and Inflation 1991 Yearbook, Copyright © 1984–1991 Ibbotson Associ-
ates, Inc. All Rights Reserved. Stocks, Bonds, and Inflation and SBBI are service marks of Ibbotson
Associates.*

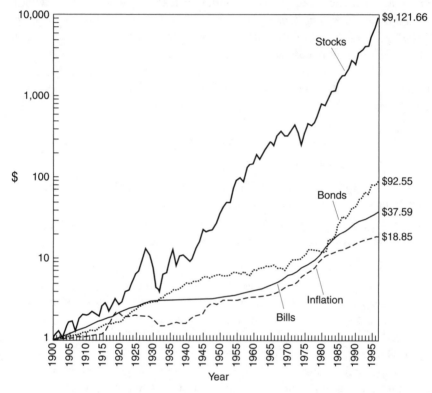

Long bonds produce higher returns, inflation-adjusted, for two reasons: Corporate bonds involve a risk of default, and both corporate and
government bonds impose on the investor an exposure to market fluctuations caused by their more distant maturity and investors "adjusting" to
changing interest rates. Investors don't want such market price fluctuations unless they get a higher rate of return to compensate, and so long
bonds pay a higher rate of interest—a *maturity premium*. The maturity
premium is estimated at 0.9 percent, and the default premium on high-
grade long-term corporate bonds works out at 0.5 percent. Adding these
two premiums to the risk-free rate, the inflation-adjusted annual real rate
of return on long government bonds is 1.0 percent, and on long corporates
it is about 1.4 percent.

Similarly, the risk premium on common stocks is calculated at 6.1 percent. (The inflation-adjusted expected *real* rate of return is, congruently, the same: 6.1 percent.)

When the powerfully disruptive impact of inflation is removed and when return experience is examined over reasonably long time periods, it becomes clear how consistent investment returns (or the returns investors require for their money) really are.

This consistency stems from two main factors:

1. Investors are sensibly consistent in requiring higher rates of return to compensate them for accepting higher market risk.

2. As the period over which returns are measured is lengthened, the short-term volatility in returns caused by changes in the discount rate becomes less and less important and the expected dividend stream, which is more stable, becomes more and more important.

The central point is that we do not have and cannot hope to get perfectly precise or "correct" data on rates of return from investments in securities any more than we can expect to get "correct" data by sampling any other complex, dynamic, continuous process that is affected by a multitude of large and small exogenous factors. However, we can get a very useful *approximation* of what returns have actually been and what they are most likely to be, and that is all we really need to establish basic investment policies for the long term.

Unless you buy in at the start of the period measured, sell out at the end, and take your money out of the market, performance data are simply hypothetical statistics. They describe samples from a continuous and very long-term process in which stock prices go through a "random walk" series of successive approximations of the actual present value of each stock based on continuously revised estimates of future earnings dividends and frequently changed discount rates.

Two further propositions on returns are important. First, the impact on returns of changes in the *expected* level of inflation can be enormous, particularly on common stocks which are virtually perpetuities. Such a change in the expected rate of inflation from approximately 2 percent in 1960 to approximately 10 percent in 1980 (along with other changes) caused a change in the required nominal average rate of return from common stocks from about 9 percent in 1960 to about 17 percent in 1980, and this produced a major reduction in stock prices. Adjusted for inflation, the loss investors experienced during that period was the worst in half a century.

A further increase in the expected rate of inflation would have further depressed stock prices. This would drop stock prices down to the level from which buyers would get sufficient returns—with the same future "real" earnings and dividends as previously expected—to offset the expected rate of inflation, compensate for risk, *and* provide a risk-free real rate of return of about 6 percent plus or minus 12 percent in two out of three years. A decrease in the expected rate of inflation would have the opposite effect, as we saw in 1982 and the following 20 years.

The second proposition on returns is that differences in rates of return that may appear moderate in the short run can, with compounding, multiply into very large and quite obvious differences in the long run. (When asked what he considered humankind's most powerful discovery, Albert Einstein allegedly replied without hesitation: "Compound interest!")[6]

When asked what he considered humankind's most powerful discovery, Albert Einstein allegedly replied without hesitation: "Compound interest."

The following table shows the compounding effect on $1.00 invested at different interest rates compounded over different periods of time (see Figure 9-2). It's well worth careful study, particularly to see how powerful *time* is. That's why time is the Archimedes' lever of investment management.

Before leaving the happy realm of investment returns, take another look at Figure 8-1, particularly the data on 25-year returns. The moderate levels of *real* returns—adjusted for inflation—are impressive and instructive: 6.6 percent on stock and 1.8 percent on bonds.

After an extraordinary quarter century of generally highly favorable investment experiences, it's useful to remind ourselves of the normal or "base rate" of investment returns.

Beware of "averages." If stocks return an average of 11 percent per year, how often over the past 75 years did stocks actually return 11 percent? Just *once*.[7] And how often did returns come close to that? In only three years did returns fall in the range of 10 to 12 percent.

---

[6]Compounding means you receive interest not only on the principal but also on the reinvested interest.

[7]In 1968.

FIGURE 9-2 Compound interest over time.

Compound Rate of Return	Investment Period		
	5 Years	10 Years	20 Years
4%	$1.22	$1.48	$ 2.19
6	1.34	1.79	2.65
8	1.47	2.16	4.66
10	1.61	2.59	6.73
12	1.76	3.11	9.65
14	1.93	3.71	13.74
16	2.10	4.41	19.46
18	2.29	5.23	27.39
20	2.49	6.19	38.34

Most investors do not want to preclude themselves arbitrarily from making the big score—the opportunity to "shoot the lights outs." If you believe with Louis Pasteur that "chance favors the prepared mind," be sure that you are prepared. First, be prepared to find nothing much. In nearly 40 years of continuous involvement with many of the world's best investors, I've found only two major opportunities; that is discovery at a rate of only once every 20 years.

If you find a great investment opportunity, what should you do? Try asking four questions and then ask other people to examine your reasoning process with you:

1. What could go really *right* and how likely is it?
2. What could go *wrong* and how likely is it?
3. Are you so confident that you plan to invest a large part of your portfolio in this one?[8]
4. If it goes down, *will you really* want to buy a lot more?

[8] My father loved bridge and played often. He was impressed one evening when his bridge partner opened with a preemptive bid: "Small slam in hearts!" He was astonished when his happy partner said, "It's a laydown!" Dad was astounded as his partner showed his hand: It was all hearts! Aghast, Dad asked the obvious question, "Why didn't you bid a *grand* slam?" He was not amused by the reply: "Because I wasn't sure how much trump support your hand would give me." Dad never fully recovered. The opportunity missed was too great to forget.

10

RISK

R *ISK IS SUCH A SIMPLE* little word that it is amazing how many different meanings are given to it by different users. (Risk is different from uncertainty: *Risk* describes the expected payoffs when their probabilities of occurrence are knowable. Actuarial mortality tables are a familiar example. The actuary does *not* know what will happen in 14 years to Mr. Frank Smith but *does* know quite precisely what to expect for a group of 100 million people *as a group*—in *each* year—including the fourteenth year.) *Riskiness* is akin to *uncertainty* in investing, and that's what the academics mean when they discuss beta and "risk." Too bad they don't use the exact terms.

Active investors typically think of risk in four different ways. One is price risk: You can lose money by buying stock at too high a price, and if you think a stock *might* be high, you know you are taking some price risk.

The second type of risk is called interest rate risk: If interest rates go up—to offset a change in expectations for inflation—more than is now expected (and already discounted in the market), your stocks will go down. You'll know you were taking risk.

The third type of risk is business risk. The company may blunder, and earnings may not develop. If this occurs, the stock will drop. Again, you were taking risk.

In the extreme, the company may fail completely. That's what happened with Equity Funding, Penn Central, and Baring Brothers and very nearly happened with IBM. As the old pros will tell you, "Now *that* is *risk!*"

They are right. But there is another way to look at risk that has come from the extensive academic research done over the past four decades; more and more investment managers and clients are using it because there's nothing as powerful as a theory that works. Here's the concept:

Investors are exposed to three kinds of investment risk. One kind of risk simply *cannot be avoided,* but investors are rewarded for taking it. Two other kinds of risk *can be avoided* or even *eliminated,* and investors are not rewarded for accepting these unnecessary and avoidable kinds of risk.

Before exploring these three quite different kinds of risk more fully—and showing how investment managers and clients can use their understanding to establish an investment policy—let's pause to show the way active investors think about risk of the kind we'll soon see is *not* rewarded.

The basic assumption of all active investors is that they will do better than the market because they will discover and exploit opportunities for profit by buying stocks that are underpriced or selling stocks or groups of stocks that are overpriced. (As explained in Chapter 1, most will be disappointed.) For investors who are competing in an intensely professionalized capital market, the additional risks, properly called "investor risks," are the risks of believing you know something special when the overwhelming odds are that what you know is not true or not correctly understood *or* is already known and has been incorporated in the market price—plus the risk of your being more emotional than rational in your investment decisions—and therefore making misjudgments.

Let's return to the theory that is powerful and useful. As was noted, all investors are exposed to three kinds of investment risk. One kind of risk cannot be avoided, but it does pay investors for taking it. Two other kinds of risk can be virtually eliminated and do not pay the person who takes them.

The risk that cannot be avoided is the risk inherent in the overall market. This market risk pervades all investments. It can be increased by selecting volatile securities or by using leverage, and it can be decreased by selecting securities with low volatility or by keeping part of a portfolio in cash equivalents. But it cannot be avoided or eliminated. It is always there. Therefore, it must be *managed.*

The two kinds of risk that can be avoided or eliminated are closely associated. One involves the risk linked to individual securities; the other involves the risk that is common to a group of securities. The first can be called individual stock risk, and the second can be called stock group risk.[1]

A few examples will clarify the meaning of stock group risk. Growth stocks as a group will move up and down in price in part because of changes in investor confidence and willingness to look more or less distantly into the future. (When investors are very confident, they will look far into the future when evaluating growth stocks.) Interest-sensitive issues such as utility and bank stocks will all be affected by changes in expected interest rates. Stocks in the same industry—autos, retailers, computers, and so forth—will share market price behavior driven by changing expectations for the industry as a whole. The number of common causes that affect groups of stocks is great, and most stocks belong simultaneously to several different groups. To avoid unnecessary complexity and to avoid triviality, portfolio managers usually focus their thinking only on major forms of stock group risk.

There are three kinds of investment risk. Two can be virtually eliminated. The third, market risk, must be managed.

The central fact about both stock group risk and individual stock risk is this: They *do not need to be accepted* by the investor. They can be eliminated. Unlike the risk of the overall market, risk that comes from investing in particular market segments or specific issues can be diversified away—to oblivion.

As a result, in an efficient market no incremental reward can or will be earned over the market rate of return simply by taking either more individual stock risk or more stock group risk. Either type of risk should be incurred only when doing so will enable the portfolio manager to make an

---

[1]Academic writers use slightly different terms to describe these three types of risk: Market risk is called *systematic risk,* individual stock risk is *specific risk,* and stock group risk is *extra market risk.* The terms used here seem clearer and more natural. Risk identified as either individual stock risk or stock group risk is the risk that the *price* of an individual stock or group of stocks will behave differently than will the overall market—either favorably or unfavorably—over the time period in which investment returns are measured.

investment that will achieve truly worthwhile increases in returns. The evidence is overwhelming that, while enticing, such ventures are not sufficiently rewarding. Yes, professional investors often are quoted as being "overweighted" in one group or another, but the fact that this is being done does not mean it is, on average, successful.

The lack of reward for taking individual stock risk or stock group risk is important because a portfolio manager who takes such risks with her clients' funds can only hope to be rewarded by her superior skill—relative to the aggregate skill of all competing investment managers—in selecting individual stocks or groups of stocks that were inappropriately priced. As was explained in Chapter 2, an investment manager who takes these risks can profit only if his competitors have made mistakes.

By assuming greater than average market risk, investors can earn greater than average returns.

Clearly, such risks can be avoided by using the simple and convenient strategy of designing a portfolio that replicates the market: no deviations in portfolio composition, no deviations in rate of return relative to the overall market, and no stock group risk or individual stock risk.

Note that eliminating these two particular forms of risk does not mean that all risk is gone. Overall market risk will always be there, and in the field of risk, that's the big one.

The great advantage of an index fund—a portfolio that replicates the overall market—is this: Such a fund provides a convenient and inexpensive way to invest in equities, with the riskiness of particular market segments and specific issues diversified away.

Risk-averse investors are willing to accept lower rates of return if they can reduce the market risks they *must* take in investing. And they are willing to see other investors get higher rates of return as an inducement to accept a larger share of the unavoidable market risk. But they will not pay their risk-taking confreres to take risks that can easily be avoided altogether by "buying the market."

Market risk is different. Because it cannot be eliminated, risk-averse investors must and will accept a less than market rate of return in order to achieve a less than market risk. By so doing, they proffer an above-average rate of return to investors who are willing to accept a greater than average market risk. This is why investors who accept more than average market risk—particularly over time—usually are rewarded with better than average market returns. (Recently, another very different kind of market risk has become a source of real concern. Overall, the stock market has risen so much that there may be an unusual but very daunting risk in the level of the whole market.)

The level of market risk taken in an equity portfolio can be estimated with good accuracy by calculating the historical price behavior of the stocks in the portfolio (on a weighted average) relative to changes in the market as a whole.[2]

The optimal level of market risk for a very long-term investor is moderately above the average. This level makes sense because many other investors are not free to take a very long-term view; their investments will be liquidated sooner—for their children's education, at the termination of a trust, or for a host of other near- to medium-term events for which plans must be made. Other investors are simply unable to look with calm forebearance on the abrupt and substantial day-to-day, month-to-month, and year-to-year changes in stock prices that will be experienced in an equity portfolio over the long term. These investors want less risk and less fluctuation and are willing to pay a price (giving up some incremental return) to get what they want.

In summary, the total return to an equity investor has four components: (1) the risk-free return, (2) an extra return to compensate for the riskiness or price uncertainty of investing in the overall equity market, (3) a potential extra return for investing in one or more particular groups of stocks or market segments that for various economic, business, or market psychology reasons may behave differently from the overall market, (4) a potential extra return for investing in specific stocks that, for the same sorts of reasons, may behave differently from the overall market.

In a similar manner, the risk accepted by the portfolio can be separated into the same kinds of component parts: risk associated with emphasis on specific stocks, risk associated with emphasis on or avoidance of particular

---

[2]The market risk inherent in investing in any single market can of course be reduced in a multi-market portfolio by balancing investments in one market with investments in other markets that behave differently. This sort of diversification is an important motivation behind the interest in investing in real estate and in diversifying internationally. The stock markets of France, Hong Kong, Japan, Italy, and Australia fluctuate as much as or more than the American market does, but usually at different times and for somewhat different reasons. The multi-market portfolio with its investment in several different markets will reduce the "unavoidable" market risk of any single market.

groups of stocks or market segments that are influenced in similar ways by common causes, and risk associated with investing in equities per se.

Thus, corresponding to each component of *return*—except the risk-free return—is a component of *risk*. Total risk consists of an overall equity market component, plus a market segment risk, plus a risk related to uncertainty about the price behavior of the stocks of individual companies relative to the overall market.

Market segment risk and specific issue risk can be diversified away, as was explained above, but overall equity market risk cannot. Figure 10-1 shows vividly how the riskiness of a single stock consists primarily of specific issue risk and market segment risk but also shows that in a typical portfolio these two kinds of risk are reduced to only a small part of the investor's total risk.

The chart also shows that the typical investor with several different managers will have even more diversification and that this degree of diver-

FIGURE 10-1   How diversification reduces nonmarket risk.

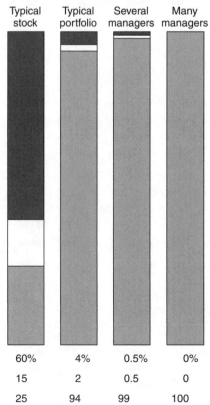

	Typical stock	Typical portfolio	Several managers	Many managers
Specific issue risk	60%	4%	0.5%	0%
Market segment risk	15	2	0.5	0
General market risk	25	94	99	100

sification will further reduce the specific issue and market segment risks to a very small percentage of total risk.

This phenomenon of very great diversification so often experienced in large funds employing several managers—usually with each manager chosen specifically because of his or her "different" style of investing but with their differences tending to cancel each other out—raises serious questions about very active management in institutional investing versus passive management with above-average market risk.

In investment management, we now know that the crucial factor is not how to manage rates of return but how to manage market risk. By managing market risk, we mean doing two things at the same time: (1) deciding deliberately what level of market risk to establish as the portfolio's basic policy and (2) holding to that chosen level of market risk. Changes in the level of market risk should be made only when there has been a deliberate change in the basic, long-term investment policy.

Managing market risk is the primary objective of investment management.

With market risk under control, you can decide whether and when to accept any individual stock risks or stock group risks in order to capture extra profits. Note that while this part of investment management gets most of the attention from investors, it is usually only a side show compared to the main force driven by the chosen level of market risk.

That managing market risk is the primary objective of investment management is a profound assertion. It is the core idea of this entire chapter. The rate of return obtained in an investment portfolio comes from three sources, in this order of importance: first and foremost, the level of market risk assumed—or avoided—in the portfolio; next, the consistency with which that risk level is maintained through market cycles; and last, the skill with which specific stock risk and stock group risk are eliminated or minimized through portfolio diversification or are well rewarded when deliberately taken.

The difference between true investment risk and apparent riskiness or market risk is a function of time. Yes, stocks can be very risky if time is short. But unless you begin your investment program at a seriously "too high" level in the stock market, when the time is long enough, the *apparent* riskiness of stocks evaporates and the favorable long-term returns become increasingly evident, as shown in Figure 10-2. For investors, the risk in investing can be divided by *time* into short-term risk and long-term risk.

FIGURE 10-2   The longer you hold stocks, the less your risk and the surer your gain.

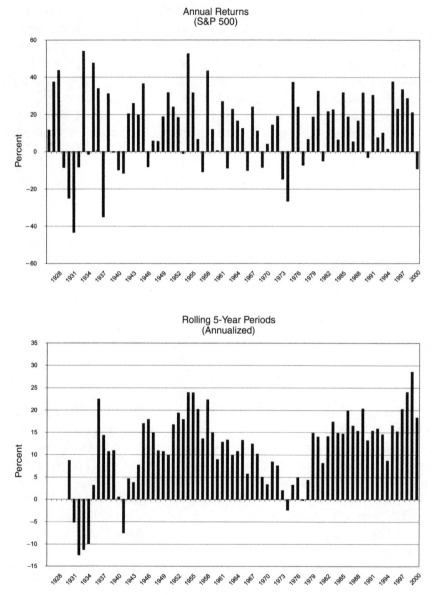

FIGURE 10-2   *Continued.*

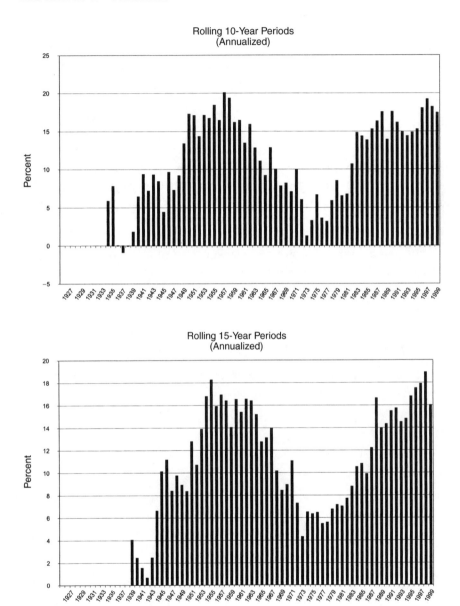

The real risk in the short term is that the investor will need to sell—to raise cash—when the market happens to be low. That's why, in the *long* term, the risks are clearly *lowest* for stocks, but in the *short* term, the risks are just as clearly *highest* for stocks. (If you do not need to sell and don't sell, you shouldn't much care about the nominal fluctuations of stock prices. They may be interesting, but they aren't any more relevant to you than is stormy weather in faraway places or low tide on the high seas.) And as we've already seen, the real risks in the long run are the risks of inflation and excessive caution.

To the extent you know your investments will be held for the very long term, you have automatically self-insured against the uncertainty of short-term market price fluctuations, because as long as you stay invested, the price fluctuations of Mr. Market just won't matter to you. The investor's best answer to short-term market riskiness is to ignore the interim fluctuations and be a long-term investor.

Recognition that risk drives returns instead of being simply a residual of the struggle for higher returns transforms the concept of investment policy.[3] We now know to focus not on rate of return but on the informed management of risk.

---

[3] As a child, I assumed that the pendulum in the grandfather's clock was driving the minute and hour hands *forward* rather than, as I later learned, holding the hands back and controlling the rate at which the weights could move them forward. For me, the concept of a clock will never be the same.

C H A P T E R

11

BUILDING PORTFOLIOS

WHETHER INVESTMENT MANAGEMENT is primarily an art or a science has long been a favorite topic of informal discussion among professional investment managers, perhaps because the discussions typically are resolved quite cheerfully by demonstrating that since the practice of investment management is clearly not a science, it therefore must be an art.

Anyone who has observed gifted investors at work will recognize the art—subtle, intuitive, complex, and usually inexplicable—in selecting individual stocks or groups of stocks. The great artists are true heroes of the profession—Phil Fisher, John Neff, Peter Lynch, John Templeton, George Soros, Warren Buffett, Howard Schow, and Rowe Price. These unusually talented investors—and others—add value to portfolios by seeing and seizing opportunities others miss or recognize only later. For these paragons there is art in stock picking.

However, for most investment managers portfolio management is neither an art nor a science. It is instead a very special problem in engineering, determining the most reliable and efficient way to reach a specified goal, given a set of policy constraints, and working within a remarkably uncertain, probabilistic, always changing world of partial information and *mis*information, all filtered through the inexact factor of human interpretation.

While the system is certainly far from perfect, recent advances in the availability of data and the development of modern portfolio theory are providing investment managers—and their more sophisticated clients—with the tools and analytical frames of reference they need to understand and define the investment problem so that it can be managed. (It would be a naive presumption to believe that the problems of managing an investment portfolio can be "solved." We must be willing to live with their being brought under reasonable control and being managed to a satisfactory standard of performance.)

An efficient portfolio maximizes expected returns at a deliberately chosen level of market risk.

As was explained in Chapter 9, we now know that the real challenge in portfolio management is not how to increase *returns*—by buying low and selling high—but how to *manage risk* by deliberately taking appropriate market risks or bets that lead predictably over time to increased returns.

The great lesson of engineering is that the key to finding the *solution* is to define the real *problem* correctly. When you have defined the problem correctly, you are well on your way to finding the correct solution for the real problem. In investing, which is *your* real problem: How to invest for the next 10, 20, or 30 *years* or how to invest for the next 10, 20, or 30 weeks? If your real problem is investing for the longer term, is your solution truly long term?

The distinctive characteristic of effective portfolio management is the elimination of *unintended* risk associated with individual stocks or groups of stocks and the deliberate assumption of intended market risk.

Although it is possible to add value through brilliant stock picking, investments in individual stocks and bonds are best thought of as components to be used in building a well-designed portfolio. They may be good components or poor components, but in the context of portfolio management individual securities have value only if they enable the investment manager to improve the portfolio as a whole by increasing the return, reducing risk, or both. Portfolio management is investment engineering.

In line with the concept of portfolio management as a challenge in engineering, the portfolio design that eliminates avoidable and unintended risk and maximizes expected returns at a deliberately chosen level of market risk is an *efficient* portfolio. An efficient portfolio has greater expected return than does any other feasible portfolio with equal risk and less risk than does any other feasible portfolio with equal expected return.

Once such an efficient portfolio has been constructed at the level of risk that is appropriate for the particular investor, it would not make sense to incur either individual stock risk or stock group risk unless such available risk were directly associated with—and judged worth taking in order to exploit—a specific opportunity to capture extra return.

The amount by which market risk and return can be magnified in a portfolio by investing in moderately higher market risk—more "price-volatile" stocks—is not spectacular, but the benefits over the very long run can be worthwhile. A portfolio with a market risk that is 20 percent greater than the overall market average is feasible. A market risk much higher than that would be difficult to design into a portfolio while keeping the portfolio well diversified. (The number and variety of stocks needed to achieve good diversification and to provide that much market risk simply are not available in the market.)

The expected "extra" rate of return for a portfolio with 20 percent more than average market risk would be, on average and over the very long term, 1.4 percentage points annually.[1] If 1.4 percentage points of incremental return over the market average return seems modest, remember that *no* sizable institutional investor has achieved that amount of annual incremental return over any sustained period of time!

Thus far, our discussion has concentrated on equity investments. Portfolio management for bonds is different in the details, but the main concepts are basically the same.

Like stocks, bonds present both individual bond risks and group risks. For example, bonds issued by companies in a particular industry will as a group change in value with major changes in that industry's economics. Bonds with particular call or refunding features in common will rise and fall as a group in relative market popularity. The normal difference in yield (and therefore price) between corporate and government bonds changes, causing larger or smaller spreads between corporates as a group and governments as a group.

It is important to note that bond rating agencies have found that most of their rating errors are caused by the difficulty inherent in estimating such group risks, not in estimating the individual risk of a particular issuer com-

---

[1]Calculated as follows: 1.2×7 percent return on equities over and above the risk-free rate of return = 1.4 percent incremental return.

pared to other issuers in the same industry or group. Therefore, diversifying across groups is important in constructing a bond portfolio.

Bond portfolio management starts conceptually with a passive portfolio that represents the overall bond market. This baseline portfolio will be diversified across numerous groups and across individual issues to protect against the credit risk of individual issuers and will use a defensive, evenly spaced schedule of maturities to defend against adverse changes in interest rates. The overall quality of the portfolio and its average maturity will be set in concert with the client's risk preferences and potential liquidity needs.

As with equities, the historical evidence is that the risk of individual bonds can be substantially eliminated through diversification with the result that portfolios of medium- to lower-grade issues do, after all actual losses through defaults on either interest or principal or both, provide higher net returns over time than do portfolios of higher-grade issues. Therefore, portfolio managers can increase risk-adjusted returns by concentrating on medium- to lower-grade bonds.

The great secret of success in long-term investing is to avoid serious losses.

Having established a well-diversified portfolio, a bond investor client can then decide whether, how, and when to deviate deliberately from the "baseline" portfolio in efforts to increase returns. There are several ways to do this:

- Buying or selling individual bonds in anticipation of an improving (or worsening) credit rating

- Switching from one bond market sector priced above its historical averages to another that is priced below its historical averages

- Selling a bond that is temporarily overpriced (perhaps because of a market imperfection) and simultaneously buying a similar bond that is underpriced (a so-called arbitrage swap)

- Changing the average maturity or duration of the entire portfolio by purchasing longer maturities (with call protection) when interest rates are expected to fall and buying shorter maturities when rates are expected to rise

However, the evidence that even professional bond managers can consistently and significantly improve results with any of these tactics is feeble. The bond markets are so efficient that even the leading professionals seldom demonstrate the ability to add enough value through active management to earn back more than the fees they charge. And those who do demonstrate superiority almost inevitably gain so much in additional assets to manage that they cannot continue to achieve superior performance. Over long periods of time, gains and losses tend to cancel each other out. How much and whether to invest in bonds at all, not which particular bonds you invest in, will be the most powerful determinant of your overall results.

Even though most investors see their work as active, assertive, and on the offensive, the reality is and should be that stock and bond investing alike are primarily a *defensive* process. The great secret of success in long-term investing is to avoid serious losses. The saddest chapters in the long history of investing are tales about investors who suffered serious losses they brought on themselves by trying too hard or by succumbing to greed. Leverage is all too often the instrument of self-destruction. Investors will be wise to remember the great difference between *maximization* and *optimization* as they decide on their long-term strategy. Icarus was a maximizer, as were many of history's destroyed "fortune builders" who "hoist themselves on their own petards [land mines]."

The basic responsibility of portfolio managers—since the invention of insurance and pooled risk accounts in merchant shipping on sailing vessels hundreds of years ago—is to control and manage risk in deliberate pursuit of wisely determined and explicitly stated objectives of the client and to limit or prevent surprises.

12

WHY POLICY
MATTERS

THE PRINCIPAL REASON you should articulate your long-term investment policy explicitly *and in writing* is to protect your portfolio from ad hoc revisions of sound long-term policy by helping you adhere to long-term policy when short-term exigencies are most distressing and your policy is most in doubt. Technology has transformed investing just as the technology of the Global Positioning System has transformed navigation. Thanks to technology, investment managers can produce—within the array of feasible results—the intended "relative-to-market" outcome for any particular portfolio. And thanks to the availability of investment technology, investors have every right to achieve results that match their expectations—and their managers' promises. Investment technology enables investment engineers to be particularly effective over long periods of time.

As a consequence, professional investment management can (and surely should) shift from short-term "conservative caution" and tactical "investment artistry" to a clear focus on explicit long-term investment policies that will achieve specified goals consistently and persistently within the investor's tolerance for interim market risk.

Bluntly, investors are now free to focus on policy and wise investment counseling, and you should hold yourself accountable for doing this essential work wisely and well—all the time.

History teaches that both investment managers and clients need help if they are to hold successfully to the discipline of long-term commitments. This means restraining yourself from reacting inappropriately to disconcerting short-term data and keeping yourself from taking those unwise actions which seem so "obvious" and urgent to optimists at market highs and to pessimists at market lows. In short, policy is the most powerful antidote to panic. The best shield for long-term policies against the outrageous attacks of acute short-term data and distress are knowledge and understanding—committed to writing. Don't trust yourself to be completely rational when all around you are driven by emotion. After all, you are human too.

Policy is the most effective antidote to panic.

The misdemeanors of investment management are almost all due to an inadequate advance understanding by investors of the *internal* realm of investor objectives or the *external* realm of capital markets and investments or both. If a major decision is truly fiduciary in nature, it never needs to be done quickly. Time-urgent decisions are *never* "fiduciary."

All too often investment policy is both vague and implicit, left to be "resolved" only in haste, when unusually distressing market conditions are putting the pressure on and when it is all too easy to make the wrong decision at the wrong time for the wrong reasons.

Such hasty reviews typically result in selling stocks—after they have dropped steeply in value—to buy into bonds and other fixed-income investments that will not rise in capital value with the next cycle of the equity market, and vice versa. Clearly, such ill-timed changes in the asset mix—selling low and buying high—can be very harmful to the long-term returns of the portfolio.

Comparable harm is done when recent returns have been higher than should be expected and investors and their professional advisers shed the requisite caution and boldly increase the amount of market risk in the portfolio (buying less seasoned and more volatile stocks). This extra portfolio risk may soon magnify the impact of a subsequent market decline, worsening the ensuing panic and leading to another round of "selling low" what investors have previously "bought high."

Investors are people and, like all people, make decisions based on their emotions when a cool, rational analysis would call for very different actions. Ironically, as human beings, investors like best those upward market movements that are most *adverse* to their long-term interests and *dislike* most those downward market movements that are in fact in their long-term interests.

As much as we may be able to see—in theory—that our long-term interests are best served by lower stock prices, who among us can honestly say that he or she does not feel a warm glow of affection for stocks and markets that have gone up even though it means stocks are now more expensive to buy and future rates of return on additional investments at these price levels will surely be lower? Who among us would close our pocketbooks and turn away from the store that puts its most attractive wares on sale at 10, 20, or even 30 percent off its recent prices? None of us would say, "I don't want to buy these things when they're on sale; I'll wait until the price goes back up and buy then." But that's exactly how we behave toward investments. When the market drops—putting stocks "on sale"—we stop buying (in fact, we even sell in a panic). And when the market rises, we buy more and more enthusiastically. As Jason Zweig puts it, "If we shopped for stocks the way we shop for socks, we'd be better off." But we are wrong when we feel good about stocks having gone up, and we are wrong when we feel bad about stocks having gone down. A falling stock market is the necessary first step to buying low.

We are wrong when we feel good about stocks having gone up a lot, and we are wrong when we feel badly about stocks that have gone down in price.

This brings us back to the main reason for studying and understanding investments and markets: to protect our portfolios from ourselves. The problem, as Santayana put it, is that "those who cannot remember the past are condemned to repeat it."

Psychologists who study anxiety and fear have found that four characteristics make people more worried about the perceived riskiness of a situation than the realities would warrant: large-scale consequences, the lack of personal control or influence, unfamiliarity, and sudden occurrence. As a result, we are more fearful of air travel (in which fewer than 30 people are killed and far fewer than 350 are hurt in a typical year) than of travel in cars (in which 30,000 people are killed yearly and well over 350,000 are injured).

Most investors experience great anxiety over large-scale, sudden, and frightening losses in portfolio value primarily because they have not been informed in advance that such events are expected and considered normal by those who have studied and understand the long history of stock markets.

Such drops in the market are—with a good understanding of market history—eminently predictable, not in their timing but in their magnitude and suddenness. And it is in these periods of anxiety—when the market has been most severely negative—that clients and managers predictably engage in ad hoc "reappraisals" of long-term investment judgment, which allows short-term fears to overwhelm the calm rationality of a long-term investment policy.

Investors need protection from their human proclivities toward unrealistic hopes and unnecessary fears—provoked by the emotionally compelling experiences of currently positive or negative surges in the market and by the current opinions that drive them. This situation is understandable. Investors who are not sufficiently informed about the true nature of investment markets do get surprised.

And investment managers are literally inundated by information in written reports; private and group meetings with corporate executives, economists, and analysts; telephone calls; stock price quotations; market transactions that give a compelling urgency to the here and now; and to what others are or may be thinking of doing. The resulting excessive attention to the present and the immediate future not only produces the "groupthink" errors explored by Gustave LeBon in his book *The Crowd* but also distracts attention from careful study of the profound difference between the short-run nature and the long-run nature of investments.

You can substantially improve your long-term portfolio returns by being sure that you are well informed about the realities of the investment environment in which your portfolio will be managed. You should carefully study the rates of return and patterns of deviation away from the averages over the past several decades, learning as thoroughly as possible why the markets moved as they did. Thoughtful, objective study of the past is the best (and also the least costly) way to develop an understanding of the basic nature of investments and markets.

As an investor, it is more rewarding to study investment history than to study the present—or various estimates of the future—so that you won't get caught in Santayana's trap of repeating the mistakes others made in the past. Visit your local library and read the financial section of your favorite magazine or newspaper for 1973, 1987, 1962, 1928, 1957, and 2000. As

Yogi Berra said, "It's déjà vu all over again." Markets always have been and always will be surprising, but there is no justification for managers or clients being amazed or shaken by any market development.

Only by understanding the nature of investing and capital markets will you escape the present paradox in which little or no attention is devoted to the truly important work of developing and adhering to wise and appropriate policies that can over time achieve realistic and relevant investment objectives and, by preventing mistakes and errors that detract from investment results, achieve superior returns.

13

THE PURPOSE
OF POLICY

THE HIGH PURPOSE OF INVESTMENT policy, and of the systematic discovery process prerequisite to it, is to establish useful guidelines for investing that are genuinely appropriate to the realities both of your own investment objectives and of the realities of the investment markets. These are the internal and external realms of investing, and investment policy must be designed to work well in both realms. In addition, good investment policies are "right" for both the long term and the many short-term periods that will be experienced in the market. Both clients and managers must be able to hold on to them even when they are most uncomfortable.

The value of a set of investment policies depends on the degree of understanding incorporated in them. First come your objectives and tolerance of risk. In institutional investment management this is the responsibility of the client to develop and of the manager to understand. Individual investors are at least responsible for clarifying their objectives and making them explicit—best done in writing—and then locating the mutual funds that truly match up with them. Second, the external realm of investments and markets is the investment professional's responsibility to understand and explain fully to you, the investor.

Understanding both dimensions of investment policy and how they can be fit together is a puzzle well worth working out. Investment policy is the explicit linkage between your long-term investment objectives and the daily work of your investment manager. If policy is *not* determined through carefully developed mutual understanding, it *will* be determined in uninformed, anecdotal "adhocracy." To the extent that you understand the realities of the situation as a whole, you will be able to understand what individual bits of data and specific events really mean—and do not mean—for the portfolio you are managing together.

Investment policy is the link between your long-term objectives and the daily work of your investment manager.

The usefulness of investment policy depends on the clarity and rigor with which investment objectives, and the policy guidelines established to achieve those objectives, are stated and consistently used.

The new language derived from modern portfolio theory makes it relatively easy to specify investment objectives and policies and to monitor portfolio operations to be sure they conform to agreed-upon policy. This language makes genuine investment counseling possible and should make it feasible for each portfolio manager to achieve excellent performance—not by heroically "beating the market" but by faithfully and sensibly carrying out realistic investment policies to achieve your stated objectives (and the different objectives of other clients).

It is now practical for you and your investment managers to agree objectively on each of these important policy dimensions:

1. The level of market risk to be taken
2. Whether the level of risk is to be sustained or varied as markets change
3. Whether individual stock risk or group risk is to be taken or avoided and the incremental rate of return which such risks, when taken, are expected to produce in the portfolio

If you wish to select an investment manager who deliberately differentiates his portfolios from the market, you must take the time to understand clearly *how* he will differentiate his portfolios (whether by betting heavily on a few stocks, by favoring a particular stock market sector, or by investing heavily in cash if he thinks stocks are overpriced), *when* he will do so (whether continually as part of a long-term strategy or occasionally as a short-term tactic), and, most important, *why* he is confident that he will achieve favorable incremental results by taking these actions.

The conceptual simplicity of setting an explicit policy on market risk and agreeing on how the portfolio will be differentiated from a fully diversified market fund is appealing in theory, but it's easier said than done. Because investing is a sampling process, as we will see in more detail in Chapter 14, performance can be measured only in probabilistic terms—in other words, manager X may be likely, but can never be certain, to approximate the market's levels of risk and return. In measuring investment portfolios, we now have good tools, but we do not have precision instruments. There are difficulties with so-called sampling errors, because companies and stocks change in terms of their investment characteristics. (Even as we strive to estimate and adjust for these changes, there will be "noise" in the data that investment managers and their clients work with.)

There are two major reasons for producing good investment policy guidelines. First in the minds of many is to have a standard by which to monitor professional investment managers. As important as this is, the other reason is paramount: to decide what your realistic long-term investment goals should be.

Time, as we have seen, is the single most important factor that separates the appropriate investment objective of one portfolio from the appropriate objective of another portfolio. Specifically, it is the length of time over which the portfolio can and will remain committed to a sustained investment policy and over which you will patiently evaluate investment results versus your objectives and policies.

Liquidity should not be given separate consideration in a well-diversified portfolio *provided* that that portfolio is invested in the kinds of securities appropriate to its time horizon. Even the largest institutional equity portfolio could easily and efficiently be liquidated in a few months. But of course, if only a year's time is available to the portfolio, it should not be invested in equities at all. It should be in money market instruments to protect the principal against unanticipatable changes in market price. Sufficient liquidity always comes along automatically when investment policy is soundly conceived and implemented.

Maintaining so-called liquidity reserves is a puzzling practice. While families, corporations, and universities naturally want to have enough cash reserves to separate their long-term investment portfolios from their operating expense budgets, cash positions within an investment portfolio should be minimized and most likely kept at zero. The basic reality of the typical pension fund is that it will have a positive cash flow from contributions every year for another generation or more and thus has no need for a liquidity reserve. Of even greater concern, many young 401(k) investors keep large proportions of their portfolios in cash even though they may be decades away from retirement.

Income requirements are excluded from this discussion of investment policy because the rate of return for an investment portfolio cannot be increased just because you want more money to spend. It is indeed a curious idea that the investment objective for a portfolio should be set according to the funds the investor wants to spend each year. Sometimes this idea shows up in pension funds where the actuarial rate of return assumption is put forth as a guide to investments. Sometimes it shows up when college presidents insist on higher endowment fund income to make up for operating deficits. And sometimes it arises when personal funds are asked to finance a more expensive way of life. In all its forms this practice is nonsense. Instead of spending decisions influencing investment decisions, it should be the other way around. Spending decisions should most definitely be governed by investment results—which follow from investment policies.

Investment policy should be separated from investment operations because they are such different responsibilities. Typically, however, responsibility for both investment policy and the operating management of the portfolio are "delegated" to professional investment managers. Mixing together investment policy and portfolio operations—problem definition and problem solving—and delegating *both* to investment managers are not appropriate.

The formulation of long-term investment policy should be clearly and explicitly separated from the operating responsibilities of portfolio management. Only by separating portfolio operations from policy formation can responsibility and accountability be established for each of these two different aspects of investment management.

Portfolio operations should clearly be the responsibility of the investment manager, but setting policy is your job. Of course, investment policy and investment management are not kept in isolation from each other. Operating performance will be evaluated objectively against the specified policy intention to be sure operations are in accord with policy, and investment policy will be evaluated objectively against long-term returns in the portfolio to be sure the policies are realistic.

If you have thoughtfully established an investment policy, you have an important advantage. You can evaluate your portfolio managers on the basis of how closely they are adhering to the strategies that will achieve your long-term policy goals. Segregating investment policy (which is your responsibility) from portfolio operations (which are the investment manager's responsibility) is the essential first step in the work of managing the managers. By obliging your investment managers to concentrate entirely on "how" while you focus on "what," you prevent their natural preoccupation with present market conditions from corrupting your portfolio's long-term policy. The time horizons of investment managers are typically shorter, often much shorter, than your time horizon as an investor. You should understand this and insist on having *your* time horizons prevail.

Having established investment objectives that are realistic in the market context and appropriate to your time horizon and your risk preferences as an investor, you should then specify the investment policies to be followed in pursuit of those stated objectives.

It is by direct comparison with these explicit investment policies—and *only* by comparison with these explicit policies—that the operational performance of the investor or professional investment manager should be measured and evaluated.

For example, it would be both unfair and misleading to attempt to evaluate the operational performance of a portfolio of growth stocks (or utility stocks, foreign stocks, or high-yield stocks) by comparing its results with the overall market averages, because such a mongrelized comparison evaluates a mixture of both policy *and* operations that should be examined separately. Specifically, the performance of a growth-stock portfolio should be critiqued in comparison with an index of growth stocks or portfolios of growth stocks. In the same way, a manager of utility stocks should be evaluated only by comparison with the investment opportunities available in utility stocks, just as the manager of a portfolio of Japanese stocks should be evaluated only in comparison with the Japanese market and not with the British, Hong Kong, or American market.

The *policy* of investing in growth stocks (or utility stocks or Japanese stocks) should be critiqued by examining the superior returns of portfolios of growth stocks (or utility stocks or Japanese stocks) in comparison with alternative types of stocks and the market as a whole over relatively long periods of time.

All too often a "growth" specialist or a "small-cap" specialist will be cheered or jeered—equally unfairly—when her type of specialty is in favor or out of favor in the overall market. In some cases a portfolio manager has been credited with "good" performance when in fact poor operational performance hindered the attainment of even higher returns that would have resulted from more carefully following an effective policy. A wise old saying goes, "Don't confuse brains with a bull market."

Just as operating performance can be evaluated against policy, policy can be evaluated against performance. If the portfolio manager does not achieve the intended investment result, should the manager be kept and the policy changed? Perhaps the objective is aimed too high. Perhaps the policy is too restrictive for the objective sought. The point is that we can learn from experience if we reflect thoughtfully on what our experience really means.

From time to time, perhaps once every two or three years, a systematic and comprehensive examination of your needs and objectives, market experience, and investment policy is appropriate. While a review of actual results could be moderately useful in critiquing policy, most of the information relevant to a basic examination of investment policy will come not from the specific portfolio but from more complete—and more relevant—analyses of major sectors of the investment market over very long periods of time.

"Don't confuse brains with a bull market."

In investing, the technology exists to identify a particular portfolio's position relative to the market, just as the Global Positioning System allows navigators to locate their actual position to within 1 meter anywhere in the world. Therefore, investors can have a "cushion for caution" against uncertainty relative to the market and can sustain long-term commitments to their long-term advantage.

If the policy is found to be inappropriate, it should be changed and the new or modified policy should be made explicit. If the operating performance of a professional portfolio manager does not conform with policy, the manager should be replaced even if his or her deviation from stated policy resulted in a higher rate of return than would have been earned by following the stated policy. (Of course, an incompetent portfolio manager would also be replaced, but this is a far easier decision to make.)

Here are a few simple tests of investment policy:

1. Is the policy carefully designed to meet your real needs and objectives?

2. Is the policy written so clearly and explicitly that a *competent stranger* could manage the portfolio and conform to your intentions?

3. Would you have been able to sustain a commitment to the policies during the most troubling capital markets that have actually been experienced over the past 50 years—when conventional wisdom was surely most opposed?

4. Would the investor or professional investment manager have been able to maintain fidelity to the policy over the same periods despite intense daily pressure?

5. Would the policy, if implemented, have achieved your objectives?

Sound investment policies will meet *all* these tests. Do yours?

14

PERFORMANCE MEASUREMENT

YOU'LL UNDERSTAND ALL YOU really need to know about the most important characteristics of the statistics of investment performance when you grasp the following concept.

If many people are in a coin-tossing contest, you can predict two results with great confidence:

1. In the long, *long* run most coin tossers will average about 50 percent heads and 50 percent tails.

2. In the *short* to intermediate term, however, some of the coin tossers will *appear* to be somewhat better than average at tossing heads—and a very few will *appear* to be much better than average at tossing heads.

If we were to inspect the record, surely the data on each individual coin tosser would be "clear and objective." But we'd know better than to think that the *past* results would be good predictors of *future* results in coin tossing. Sooner or later each of the coin tossers would become more and more *average*. Statisticians call this powerful yet common phenomenon *regression to the mean*. Understanding the determining power of regression to the mean is the key to understanding a lot about reported investment performance.

Performance measurement is least useful when it is needed most—and is needed least when it could be most effective.[1] This chapter explains why.

As a professional investment manager is given more and more discretion to deviate from a market fund and take more and more risks of different kinds—market risk, group risk, and individual stock risk—the difficulty of determining how much of any specific period's portfolio return is due to skill versus chance increases rapidly.

Performance data that are sufficiently timely to have relevance for practical decisions on how well a manager is really doing and whether a manager should be changed are based on too small a sample or too short a time period to provide enough information to make an accurate decision. And results for longer time periods—which offer greater accuracy—are not sufficiently timely to be relevant for current decisions on how well managers are doing unless the results are overwhelmingly good or bad.

Measurements of investment performance do not, at least in the short run, "mean what they say." Performance measurement services do not report "results." They report statistics. As usually reported in their two-decimal form for a known time period, investment returns sound almost microscopically accurate: "Over the 12 months ending June 30, manager A returned 27.53 percent." That apparent precision gives such performance numbers an apparent legitimacy they do not deserve since they are in truth a sampling—not a measurement—of investment returns.

By expressing recent short-term returns in such precise terms, performance measurement turns our heads: It makes us believe that the short term is meaningful and that the long term will resemble it. There is a strong human tendency to think about the phenomenon being measured in the time interval used and let the measurement interval dominate the time horizon that actually should be used. However, we all know that short-term thinking is the mortal enemy of long-term investment success.

These statistics are arbitrary samples drawn period by period from a most unusual and continuous process—the process of managing complex, changing portfolios of securities in the context of a large, dynamic, always changing, and often turbulent free and competitive capital market. The stocks and bonds in the portfolios are frequently changed, companies and their businesses are always changing in many different ways, and the factors that most affect the prices of securities (fear, greed, inflation, poli-

---

[1] Professor Barr Rosenberg estimates that it would require 70 years of observations to show conclusively that even 200 basis points of incremental annual return resulted from superior investment management *skill* rather than chance.

tics, economic news, business profits, investors' expectations, and so forth) never cease to change.

As long as the portfolio is not being cashed in, this multidimensional set of change forces will go on and on revising the value of the portfolio. There are no real "results" until the process stops and the portfolio is finally liquidated. Regression to the mean is a central reality in the pattern so frequently observed in long data time series (such as investment management and coin tossing). The manager whose favorable investment performance in the recent past *appears* to be "proving" that he or she is a better manager is often—not always, but all too often—about to produce *below-average* results. Why? Usually, a large part of the apparently "superior" performance was *not* due to superior skill that will continue to produce superior results but instead was due to that particular manager's sector of the market enjoying above-average rates of return—or luck. However, when the tide turns, the behavior of the segment of the market that propelled the manager ahead may hold him or her back. That's one reason why investment managers' results so often regress to the mean. Another reason is this: With so many professional managers being so good at what they do, it is difficult to beat the crowd because the crowd is full of *professionals* who work very hard and are always striving to be better. And these professionals play the game very, very well.

Long-term performance data also have a "survivor" bias *and* a "new-firm" bias. Here's why. New investment management firms are launched by managers who can show off the superior results they have achieved in recent years, often with a previous employer. Firms that continue to get good results typically take on more new accounts, while older firms that *appear* to have poor performance may lose accounts. Those with the worst results go out of business. (As in any field, the doctors bury their mistakes.) Thus, the average manager in business today will have slightly better performance than the average manager who was in business 25 or 50 years ago. And advertising will be touting the managers with the "best records," and so investors will hear most often from those who've been the most successful—so far.

Statisticians debate among themselves whether it takes 40, 60, or 80 years to determine definitively whether the incremental return obtained by a particular portfolio is attributable to luck or to skill. Of course, the debate is academic because almost no investment manager has reliable performance data going back 40 or 60 years. Moreover, by the time performance data are good enough for investors to act with confidence on the conclusion, the optimal time for action will be long past.

Since each investment manager's actual performance will—like the market's return—be drawn from a bell-shaped probability distribution around a mean or average annual rate of return, investment objectives and performance measurements should be understood and specified in terms of both the mean or average rate of return (also known as "the base rate" or normal rate of return) and the distribution around that mean.

Recognizing that measurements of performance are statistics leads to an appreciation that as with any series of statistics, each data point must be read not as an exact number but only as an *approximation* of an exact number.

For users of performance measurement, the big problem is separating three very different factors that are mixed into the overall performance data. One factor is the "sampling error," or the probability that the statistics do not precisely equal the facts. As in any sample, there will be imprecision or uncertainty. In investment performance data, the sampling error is the degree to which the particular portfolio, for the particular time period, is or is not a good representative sample of the manager's work.

The second factor is that during the measurement period, the market conditions may have been a favorable or unfavorable environment for the particular manager's way of investing. For example, investors in small-capitalization stocks have had both very favorable and very unfavorable market environments during the past decades. As a result, they have all looked better than they really were in some years and looked worse than they really were in other periods. This is why most investment managers should be measured over at least one full cycle of up markets and down markets.

The third factor is the skill—or *lack* of skill—of the investment manager. This is what many clients and managers most want to measure. But here's the rub: In the very short run sampling errors will have a much larger impact on the measured results than will the manager's skill.

To be specific, it would not be at all unusual for an investment manager's results to be in a range that was within 2 percent of the return that would be expected most of the time from a broadly diversified portfolio with the same level of market risk. As was noted earlier, it would take many years of performance measurement to know whether the *apparently* superior results were due to the manager's skill or to good luck. By the time you had gathered enough data to determine whether your manager really was skillful or just lucky, at least one of you would probably have died of old age. The impossibility of using short-term or even intermediate-term performance measurement to manage managers by acting on "results" is what makes it essential that clients and investment managers establish and sustain wise long-term investment policies.

One thing is certain: You should insist on full disclosure of the performance of *all* the manager's portfolios so that you can get a good sample of the manager's *overall* achievement. You should not try to infer a professional manager's overall performance from your own portfolio—a sample of one!

For you, a key problem lies in deciding how to interpret the results. Should you accept the manager's assurances that below-average results will surely be reversed in the coming period and that you should stay? Or should you reject the assurance, assert that the manager is "out of control," and terminate the relationship?

The power of regression to the mean in investing is illuminated in Figure 14-1. Each column shows—for each quintile—the average annual compound returns achieved by investing with *last* year's quintile-by-quintile managers for the *next* year. The final column shows the 10-year cumulative average. Even a brief inspection of the annual columns—particularly the 10-year final column—shows that *past performance does not predict future performance.*

Most individual investors are aware of the ubiquitous ratings of mutual fund performance coming from Morningstar. But how many investors know that Morningstar quietly acknowledges that its "one-star" to "five-star" ratings report only a fund's one-year *past* performance relative not to the particular fund's legitimate peer group but to *all* funds despite their considerable differences in policy and style mandate? Serious investors know

FIGURE 14-1   Subsequent-year median annual returns for managers, sorted by past year's returns.

Source: *Cambridge Associates.*

Performance Quintile	1990	1991	1992	1993	1994	1995	1996	1997	1998	1999	10-Year Average
First	40.5	7.2	18.3	−0.2	35.5	23.6	32.2	25.4	34.3	−12.2	19.3
Second	36.8	8.8	15.3	0.1	35.8	24.1	31.4	26.8	21.0	−7.1	18.4
Third	32.9	9.7	13.2	0.2	35.0	22.9	30.5	17.5	20.7	0.3	17.7
Fourth	32.2	9.7	11.0	1.0	36.4	22.8	30.0	18.8	8.2	5.9	17.0
Fifth	31.9	10.9	11.2	1.7	32.8	19.8	27.0	16.0	9.2	12.7	16.9

Notes: Results show the 10-year average annual compound returns achieved by investing in a given quintile's median manager for 1-year periods over the past 10 years ending December 31, 2000.

that performance in the recent past is not predictive of the future and that one year is much too short a period for evaluating investing capabilities. In plain English, the most widely recognized ratings are worthless for making investment decisions.

Morningstar candidly admits that its star ratings have *zero* predictive power, yet 100 percent of net new investment money going into mutual funds goes to "five-star" and "four-star" mutual funds. (We've all seen the numerous ads trumpeting the high ratings.)

However, unintentionally, Morningstar ratings are misleading investors. *After* the ratings are handed out each year, the "five-star" funds—despite 25 percent greater volatility—generally earn less than half as much as the broad market index. Growth stock funds clearly outperformed the market in the late 1990s, but Morningstar's rating in 1996—when the superior results of "growth" were beginning—was a "below-average" 2.8 stars. (By 2000, when it was too late to be buying "growth," its rating had moved up to more than four stars.) And the top quartile funds of the 1980s—when their results were 2.8 percent ahead of the market—*lost* 1.7 percent relative to the market per year in the 1990s. Don't you wish Morningstar would make sure this reality is widely understood?

It would take many years of measurement to determine if a portfolio manager's "superior" results were due to skill or luck.

Take a careful look at the data in Figure 14-1. As you'll soon see, there's nothing to see. *There is no pattern*. Like Sherlock Holmes's dog that didn't bark, this lack of pattern *is* the pattern. As Gertrude Stein once said in dismissing the possibility of visiting a particular city: "There's no *there* there."

The grievous lack of "predictability" of *future* performance on the basis of past performance is shown in Figure 14-2, a stunning comparison of results for the top 20 performers in a recent *bull* market and the results for the same funds the very next year in a *bear* market.

This "now you see it, now you don't" was first and most delightfully shown for individual common stocks by Ian M. D. Little, the investment bursar of Nuffield College at Oxford, in his delightful, enthralling essay "Higgledy, Piggledy, Growth."

FIGURE 14-2   Comparative fund performance in successive bull and bear markets.

Rank in Bull Market*	Rank in Bear Market*
1	3,784
2	277
3	3,892
4	3,527
5	3,867
6	2,294
7	3,802
8	3,815
9	3,868
10	3,453
11	3,881
12	3,603
13	3,785
14	3,891
15	1,206
16	2,951
17	2,770
18	3,871
19	3,522
20	3,566

*Rank among 3,896 mutual funds in performances during the 12 months ending on March 30, 2000, and the 12 months ending on March 30, 2001.

With most of the buying and selling in the stock and bond markets now being done by professionals, the pricing mechanism is what statisticians would describe as open and fair. (Rough, perhaps *very* rough—particularly on amateurs—but statistically fair all the same.) As a result of their intensive competition, it is very hard for any one institution to get much ahead of the competition and even harder for it to stay ahead.

Thus, over very long periods, the median or average return obtained by most professional investors would be expected to be close to the market average (such as the S&P 500) *minus* at least 1 percent of operating costs each year for advisory fees and commissions on transactions and custody expenses. The professionals would be expected to lag *behind* the market (as was explained in Chapter 1), and this is what studies of investment performance consistently show. The average professionally managed fund has a rate of return approximately equal to that of the market *minus* the costs to participate in the market. How could it be otherwise? The professionals *are* the market.

Over the past 50 years, mutual funds have lost 180 basis points—compounded annually—compared to the S&P 500.[2] As a result of intensive competition, it is very difficult for any one institution to get ahead of the professional competition and *stay* ahead. That's why most institutions' long-term performance clusters near—but below—the market average. In the past 30 years, mutual funds have had the long-term results relative to the overall stock market shown in Figure 14-3.

The dominant realities are clear: Nearly three-quarters of the mutual funds—16 percent plus 57 percent—achieved market performance or *less* than market performance, and only 2 percent of the funds were more than 2 percent ahead of the market over the whole period. (And that's before taxes.) While understandable and even predictable, this record is *not* encouraging news for investors who want to believe in investing in actively managed mutual funds.

Even more disconcerting for mutual fund investors, the average mutual fund *investor* gets a return that is significantly *below* the return of the average mutual fund.[3] From 1984 to 1995 the investors' shortfall was a stunning

FIGURE 14-3   Long-term performance of mutual funds versus the market.

Proportion of Funds	Performance versus Market
16%	2% or worse
57	0 to −2%
26	0 to 2%
2	2% or more

[2]John C. Bogle, "The Clash of Cultures in Investing: Complexity vs. Simplicity." Speech given for the Money Show, Orlando, Florida, February 3, 1999.

[3]Gary Belsky and Thomas Gilovich, *Why Smart People Make Big Money Mistakes* (New York, Simon & Schuster), p. 178.

6 percent annually, almost one-half of the 12.3 percent "earned" by the average equity mutual fund. Even investors in *bond* funds got less than their funds did: only 8 percent versus 9 percent. A 1999 study[4] concluded that while the S&P 500 gained an average of 17.9 percent a year over the 15 years from 1984 to 1998, the typical investor in stock funds earned only 7 percent a year over that period. The reason: frequent trading or turnover. Instead of staying the course with their investments, many investors tried to time the market, holding a fund for less than three years before selling and buying something else.

If the income tax consequences of what has become "typical" portfolio turnover—100 percent or more annually—are deducted, mutual fund performance gets cut back even more: typically by more than 3 percent.

Now, if only 2 percent of mutual funds are significantly "above market" and if you share the view that finding the really right *two* in a hundred is not a good "game" to play with real money, surely you will also agree that there is one fine alternative, index funds, where income taxes are far lower because turnover is far lower.

The odds of outperforming the market get worse and worse as the measurement period gets longer and longer—and more significant— as shown in Figure 14-4. (A separate study by Lipper and Company found that only 13.25 percent of surviving mutual funds beat the S&P 500. Note the qualifying term *surviving*. Even mutual fund companies "bury their mistakes.")

A major problem for investment managers and for their clients is the considerable dispersion in the performance being produced by the same investment managers when managing portfolios with the same investment policies. The results should be the same, but the differences can and often

FIGURE 14-4   Very long-term performance of mutual funds versus the market.

Period of Time	Percentage of Funds Outperforming the Market
1 year	35
10 years	25
25 years	10
50 years	5

[4]Dalbar, Inc.

will be substantial. For an investment manager, such dispersion is clearly an important problem in quality control.

Information is data with a purpose. Because performance measurement can be useful only when a valid standard has been clearly established, performance measurement depends on a clear and explicit investment policy. And the purpose of regular measurements of portfolio performance must be to determine whether current portfolio *operations* are in faithful accord with long-term *policy.*

Performance measurement cannot and will not be useful in measuring results. Only an approximate answer can be given to a question such as "What rate of return was earned in this quarter?" and that approximation will not be useful unless the results for such a short period are extreme. However, quite useful information can be drawn from performance measurement on the investment *process.* If portfolio operations have not been in accord with agreed policy and the investment manager's agreed-upon mission, it is not really important whether current portfolio results happen to be above (lucky you) or below (unlucky you) the results that would be expected if the policy had been followed faithfully. In either case the truly important information is that the portfolio and the portfolio manager are out of conformance and may be out of control. Sooner or later this lack of control will show up in losses—uncontrolled and unrecoverable losses.

There are other practical problems with performance measurement, particularly when it is used to measure whether a portfolio is or is not "within policy."

First, estimates of the risk of individual stocks and the risks of groups of stocks are estimates of probable *future* price behavior based on the best available estimates of *past* behavior. While past patterns of behavior are usually the best available guide to likely future patterns, the future is sure to differ in significant measure from the past.

Second, the relationship between the "market" and a specific stock or portfolio of stocks is not constant. This relationship "drifts." Consequently, the past will not be a perfectly reliable basis on which to estimate the current or the future "relative" behavior of a stock or group of stocks.

Third, the amount of "drift" in the relationship over time will be less for stocks of major companies in established industries and will be more for stocks in small or marginally successful companies, particularly in rapidly changing industries.

Fourth, even the most rigorous statistical descriptions of individual stocks or groups of stocks are themselves estimates and are stated in terms of statistical probabilities, with the implicit understanding that there will be a distribution of actual experience around the expected mean.

Fifth, just one or two decisions—perhaps brilliantly skillful, perhaps lucky, perhaps both—can make a powerful difference in the reported performance of a portfolio.[5] Professional investment managers will recognize how often one of their portfolios has enjoyed far better results than another portfolio simply because, when implementing a strategic decision to invest heavily in a particular industry group, the stock used in one portfolio did very well while the stock used in another portfolio did badly.

Sixth and most important is the problem of "end period dominance." Almost always, the most important factor in the reported performance of an investor or a professional investment manager is not his or her skill but the choice of starting date and ending date. Many of the most impressive "gee whiz" charts of investment performance become quite ordinary by simply adding or subtracting one year at the start or the end of the period shown.

More and more investors (and all professional investment managers) are properly dissatisfied with the convention of comparing the results of their portfolio to the results of a group of other portfolios of similar size, even though these portfolios do not have the same long-term investment policies. The most effective and informative use of investment performance data is to determine not whether a manager's portfolio performance is superior or inferior, but whether a manager is conforming to his or her promised and expected mission. A *value* stock manager should be producing good results relative to value stocks; a growth manager should be producing good results relative to growth stocks. A portfolio's operations should only be judged in comparison with its policy commitment and the results that should reasonably be expected given that policy, *or* in comparison to a peer group of funds with the same investment objective and with a similar prescribed level of market risk. One of the key criteria on which performance should be measured is this: Did the portfolio manager keep the portfolio's market risk at the level specified in the statement of investment policy?

In addition, it would be more equitable and more informative to compare a portfolio's results with those of other portfolios with a similar mission:

[5]The classic example was the impact of a spectacularly successful but small and almost accidentally made investment in Digital Equipment (actually made as a matter of *noblesse oblige* honor—a single "start-up" technology company because an MIT professor had said he thought he had been promised financial support). With it, American Research and Development (AR&D, a venture capital fund) significantly outperformed the market averages. Without Digital, AR&D would have underperformed the market during its 20-year life—before any adjustment for risk or illiquidity.

growth-stock portfolios versus growth-stock portfolios, conservative-stock portfolios versus conservative-stock portfolios, "small-cap" stock portfolios versus "small-cap" stock portfolios, and so on.

In the same vein, the performance of an equity portfolio should be based on the total assets available for equity investment, not just the portion that happened to be in stocks—with cash "reserve" positions excluded. The same applies to bond portfolios: Cash reserves should be counted in, not counted out. (Whether the use of cash reserves helped or hurt performance compared with a fully invested portfolio can and should be examined separately.)

For balanced accounts, the equity portfolio (cash reserves included) should be measured in comparison to similar equity funds, the bond portfolio (cash reserves included) should be compared to similar bond funds, and the impact of shifts in the stock/bond mix should be reported and examined separately to see whether these shifts in asset mix are contributing to overall results.

One of the great frustrations thoughtful investment professionals have had with typical performance measurement is that bad decisions with favorable outcomes are often well received by innocent clients while good decisions with temporarily unfavorable outcomes can lead to the loss of an account. Variances from expected and intended results are just as "wrong" when the apparent result is *above* expectation as they are when the result is *below* expectation. (A ship is just as far off course when it is 10 miles *west* of its objective as when it is 10 miles *east* of its objective.) Sure, it's nice for the investor to get a higher return than a lower return, but either one is "off target," and the investor should not confuse good luck (or bad luck) with the manager's skill.

Portfolios should be compared with portfolios with a similar mission, such as growth versus growth or small cap versus small cap.

More serious—because it is more common—is the pattern of clients choosing managers just after they have had "their kind of market" and imputing to these managers a special set of skills and genius that will be impossible to sustain after that market environment changes.

For example, a "growth" manager may outperform other growth managers only to have some clients terminate their accounts because the results were below the returns earned over the same period by "value" managers when the prices of value stocks were doing particularly well.

The final problem with performance measurement is its perverse tendency to stimulate counterproductive thinking and behavior by diverting your interest and attention to short-term operating results and away from long-term policy. The process of measuring almost certainly influences the phenomenon being measured, as the physicist Heisenberg elucidated years ago with his "principle of indeterminacy." As usually reported in their two-decimal form for a known time period, investment returns sound almost microscopically accurate: "Over the 12 months ending June 30, manager A returned 27.53 percent." That apparent precision gives such performance numbers a legitimacy they do not deserve, since they are in truth a sampling, not a measurement, of investment returns.

By expressing recent short-term returns in such precise terms, performance measurement turns our heads: It makes us believe that the short term is meaningful and that the long term will resemble it. There is a strong human tendency to think about the phenomenon being measured in the time interval used in the measuring and to let the measurement interval dominate the time horizon that actually should be used. But we all know that short-term thinking is the mortal enemy of long-term investment success.

A form of Gresham's law ("bad money drives out good") can easily take over as portfolio managers and investors alike allow the obsession with short-term performance to drive out the thoughtful concern with longer-term policy objectives. (Quarterly performance, as we've just discussed, really can't be "measured" very accurately, although it certainly can be reported with apparent "precision." The sample is too small to give useful information.) This can easily lead to a series of constant adjustments to long-term policy in an effort to improve short-term performance. The tail (short-term performance) should not be allowed to wag the dog (long-term policy).

The main reason for measuring performance is to improve investor-manager communication and vice versa. The purpose of performance measurement is not to provide answers but to identify questions that investors and managers should explore together to be sure they have a good mutual understanding of what is contributing to and what is detracting from investment performance. Ask the child's favorite series of questions: Why? Why? Why?

Central to good investor-manager communication is information that shows whether the portfolio is being managed in accordance with agreed-upon policy, particularly policy on market risk and on the type of investments in which the manager is expected to specialize. The impact of these two policy parameters should be measured and reported on a regular basis. The better mutual funds do this.

The key concept is this: *Any unexpected and unexplained deviation from realistic expectation is poor performance.* (A sensible proxy for "realistic expectations" of a mutual fund is the average performance of other funds with similar investment objectives.) A *large* unexplained deviation is *very* poor performance. And as every user of the statistical techniques of quality control[6] knows, it makes *no difference* whether the deviation is *above* or *below* expectation. Sure, we investors are trained to think that higher returns are better returns, and in the long run they certainly are. But in the shorter run, deviating above *or* below expectation indicates that the manager is out of conformance to his or her mission. And "out of conformance" usually means out of control[7]—with unhappy results the very probable eventual outcome.

The final area of "performance measurement" is clearly qualitative. Does the manager's explanation of his or her decisions make good sense? Is the manager doing as promised—making the kinds of decisions that were "advertised"? Are the manager's actions consistent with his or her words at the previous meeting? When the manager changes the portfolio's structure, do the explanations make good common sense? As a thoughtful, interested client, do you find your confidence in the manager's abilities, knowledge, and judgment rising as you have more and more discussions—or is it falling?

Investors should give real weight to these "soft" qualitative factors because over and over again, this is where the best signals of real trouble first surface, long before the problem is evident in the "hard" quantitative data.

Even more important, sophisticated investors have been able to stay with professional managers who made good qualitative sense even when

---

[6]Deming and Juran built great careers helping manufacturers achieve superior product quality through such statistical techniques for analyzing consistency and conformance to plan and intention.

[7]Investors might think of performance in driving. Swerving off the road to the right is just as badly out of control as swerving off the road to the left. It's the same with investment performance.

the quantitative measures of performance were "disappointing" because a manager was conscientiously and competently following her agreed-upon mandate even though that mandate happened to be temporarily out of tune with the market's favorite sectors. In many cases the subsequent performance has been very rewarding to both manager and client. In fact, a good test of the care with which a client has chosen a manager would be this: If the manager underperformed the market because his or her particular style was out of favor, albeit skillfully implemented, would you cheerfully assign substantially *more* funds to the manager? If your answer is yes, it would be because you would recognize that the manager will outperform the overall market averages when investment fashion again favors his or her style. This is the favorable side of regression to the mean, so why not take advantage of it?

15

MANAGING
MANAGERS

VERY FEW INVESTMENT MANAGERS and very few investor clients are fully satisfied with their present relationships, and it's their own fault. Too little attention is devoted by either clients or managers to designing and developing truly successful relationships. While investment managers can be faulted for not taking more initiative in this area, the primary responsibility rests and always will rest with the clients.

Great clients make great firms, and the clients of investment managers can do a real service for their managers by combining three attributes: rigorous insistence on adherence to the explicitly agreed-upon mission, candor in discussing areas of dissatisfaction or uncertainty, and patience with the understandably human nature of investment managers—encouraging the glum and disappointed and cautioning the euphoric and self-assured.

Clients should assert themselves in developing good working relationships with investment managers for several reasons. First, as was discussed in Chapter 1, as a client you know (or certainly ought to know) what is unusual and important about your investment objectives. It is your responsibility as a good client to project this knowledge into the process of formulating long-term objectives and an investment policy.

Second, investment managers are so deeply immersed in the demanding details of daily investment operations that it is implausible for them—

alone and unaided—to find the time and interest to think through the specific circumstances of every client and develop sensitively separate policies for each one.

Third, the real need in most investment relationships is not for more *investment* management but for more *management* management. This set of skills is far more likely to be found among corporate executives, foundation trustees, and makers of trusts with general management experience and orientation than among investment management specialists.

Finally, you as the client have the most to gain from developing successful and purposeful relationships. While the manager can lose the account, his or her downside risk is the loss of a fee; as a client your downside risk is no less than the health of your whole portfolio.

How many different investment managers should you use? With mutual funds, an investor usually can find several different *styles* or concepts of investing offered by one major family of funds. All the funds offered by a family will be organizationally accountable for the same standards of professionalism, reasonable fees, and investor services. That's why it makes sense to concentrate on one or two fund families whose long-term investment results and business values and practices you respect.[1]

Here are some suggestions on how to be a good client. They work well for institutional investors and are well worth consideration by all individual investors. First, start by knowing what your own investment objectives and staying power really are. You should study your own record of decisions over the years to see how well you perform as a client and, in particular, examine your capacity to tolerate investment adversity in different time frames. For example, it's one thing to know your ability to handle what might be called quarter-to-quarter fluctuations: They are usually relatively modest and soon are reversed. It's another thing to absorb and accept a full bear market, particularly one that lasts longer and plummets more than normal; for example, ask how you would feel if stocks lost more than 37 percent of their value, as the S&P 500 did in 1973–1974, shrinking $1,000 to less than $630 in two awful years. (Unlisted stocks lost even more, over 75 percent.)

The perspective from which to test yourself is not the calm armchair of the market historian who can see "how it all worked out" in the end. Instead, you'll want to think very carefully about the way you would really

[1] If in doubt, ask your employer's pension executive or your accountant for the names of a few organizations he or she respects the most for *very* long-term investment, write for the literature on *all* their funds and their organizations, study this information carefully, and then make your own final selection. Discipline your decision making with the determination to stay invested for the very long term.

feel and might react to the dreadful experience of a severe bear market at its worst moment, when the next stage is not known and may be even worse! This kind of candid self-critique will help you determine your true investment staying power.

Determining your tolerance for pain and investment staying power will provide you with the basis on which you can set the level of market risk that you can and will live with. Don't overcommit. Know your internal realities and stay within your own limitations. As my father wisely advised: "Never risk more than you know you can afford to lose."

"Never risk more than you know you can afford to lose."

Second, learn to understand the *external* realities of the investment markets and do not expect more of your managers than they can deliver. If you insist on "beat the market" performance, you *will* find managers who will make that promise. But can they really keep it?

Third, select managers who are clearly competent to complete the mission you have in mind for them, who understand the mission and accept it, and with whom you would genuinely enjoy working. A good rule that is simple to state but very difficult to follow for most investors is this: Never choose a manager you would not confidently "double up" with *if* the manager's current performance was significantly off the market for a year or so *and* popular opinion was saying that the manager had lost his touch.

Finally, strive to discipline yourself to keep faith with your own commitment to a steady, long-term program. Follow the advice of Caesar: *De minimus non curat praetor!* (Don't be concerned with small matters!)

Changing investment managers without good cause is a lot like market timing. The experience of most investors who change managers is poor: They lose money. The main features of mutually advantageous manager-client relationships are not difficult to describe. First, the relationship should be designed and intended to last a long time. Changing managers is costly and disruptive for both the manager and the client and usually comes only after an unhappy series of misunderstandings and mistakes leads to endemic mistrust.

As in any good business relationship, the responsibilities and undertakings of each party should be both realistic and clear. In particular, the investment manager's "mission" should be both explicit and in writing and should be mutually agreed upon. It should be within the competence of the investment manager, should be realistic and reasonable relative to the market, and should satisfy your legitimate and informed expectations. If these three criteria are *not* being met, the client should get together with the investment manager until they have agreed on a mission statement that passes all three tests.

Second, the relationship usually will be centered on quarterly or semi-annual meetings organized to achieve the success in working together desired by both the investment manager and the client. Before each meeting, an agenda should be prepared by the client and all relevant documentation should be provided, usually by the manager, with ample time for careful preparation by both the manager and the client. (The emphasis on *relevant* documentation is deliberate: It takes little genius to flood a meeting with enough trivia to camouflage the central issues.)

The investment manager's "mission" should be both explicit and in writing —and mutually agreed upon.

Each meeting should begin with a careful review of the investment manager's mission—the agreed-upon investment policies of the portfolio through which the manager is expected to accomplish the mutually intended long-term objective—to see if any modification in either objective or policy is appropriate. If they have no changes in mission to propose, both the client and the investment manager should explicitly reaffirm the mission statement. If either the client or the manager wishes to propose a change, the proposal and the rationale supporting it should be prepared in advance and distributed as one of the meeting preparation documents so that all participants can study and think through the proposed change. There should, of course, be no surprises in this most important part of the meeting.

Discussion of specific portfolio operations—purchases and sales of specific securities—should be on an exception basis and should be brief. This portion of the meeting should *not* be "interesting." Clients should not accept colorful recitations of war stories or capsule reviews of specific stocks: They are fun, but they are only entertainment. Instead, this part of the meeting should be a straightforward confirmation that the manager has sensibly and faithfully followed an agreed-upon policy. Like a successful medical examination, the review of operations should be thorough and expeditious and should conclude with the assurance, "As expected, we are achieving your objectives with the concepts and process we promised to use in managing your investments, and everything is fine."

At most, the review of operations and reaffirmation of the investment manager's mission should take just 10 minutes. If it takes longer, "Houston, we have a problem." Something is wrong: Either the mission is not clear, or the results are "off mission." The balance of the meeting time, usually another half hour, can best be devoted to a thoughtful and detailed discussion of almost any topic of importance to both the client and the manager as a way to increase shared understanding.

At least once a year the main topic should be a candid review—led by the *client*—of the client's overall financial situation and the context in which the investment portfolio fits.

Similarly, for institutional investors it will usually be relevant for the investment manager to devote the balance of the meeting to a discussion of his organization's professional and business development—with particular emphasis on the investment management firm's long-term business and professional policies and commitments—and the importance to his firm of the kind of account represented by the client. For individual investors, a written description of the manager's desired clientele and the service for which the manager intends to be accountable can be useful.

Other meetings can constructively be devoted to discussions of a major economic development, a major portfolio commitment, or the changing economics or investment attraction of a particular industry. The important purpose of these topical discussions is to enable the client to take a deep look into the thinking process of the investment managers.

Meetings should *not* be used as they almost always are: for a brief tour of the investment world that might include superficial comments on the economic outlook, recent changes in interest rates, a review of minor changes in the weightings of industry groups in the equity portfolio, and a quick recap of modest shifts in quality ratings in the bond portfolio, concluding with some interesting insights into specific decisions.

Such discussions are just entertainment and can easily deteriorate into a superficial "show and tell" report of current events. Without really digging into any of the major decisions made, they can use up time that otherwise might be devoted to serious discussions of subjects of potentially enduring importance to a successful relationship—and to the portfolio.

A written summary of perhaps three to five pages should be prepared and distributed after each meeting and kept for future reference. One good suggestion would be to have alternating meetings summarized by the client and the investment manager.

Meetings should not be used to bring new members of the client's investment committee up to date. Such catch-up briefings should be conducted separately, perhaps earlier on the day of the main meeting. With a good written record of each prior meeting, these catch-up briefings can be accomplished both quickly and reliably—to everyone's benefit.

Three functions can be served by an investment committee, and experience suggests that they can be served best when they are carefully *separated*. The three functions are as follows:

1. Determining *investment policy* for the whole fund over the very long term—focusing on the long-term asset mix, the intended market, riskiness, and so forth, and making careful, documented, and explicit judgments about what's "right" for the particular fund and feasible for long-term investment in the capital markets.

2. Dividing the total portfolio's overall investment policy into specific assignments for each of the fund's different investment managers so that each one will have agreed-upon defined benchmarks or "normal" portfolios with agreed-upon expectations for investment results in various market scenarios.

3. Evaluating the period-to-period effectiveness with which each investment manager is performing in meeting that manager's specific agreed-upon assignment.

The meeting's agenda for decisions to be made would match *each* of these three functions:

1. Is the asset mix "right" for this particular fund *and* feasible over the very long term? (Or to put it the other way around, is there a compelling near-term reason to change the previously "right" long-term policy to a *new* "right" long-term policy?)

    Since changes in a pension plan's or an endowment's needs or even in a typical individual's situation—*or* changes in the basic nature of the capital markets—usually develop only gradually, decisions to change an investment policy seldom are made. They *might* be given careful review once a year; they should be reviewed carefully after any *major* change in the needs of the investor.

2. Given the overall investment policy—after making any sound, long-term adjustment—would it make sense to make any changes in the assignments given to specific managers? Again, change is unlikely and should be infrequent.

3.   Given performance relative to agreed-upon benchmarks *or* changes in the client's assessment of each manager's capabilities to perform the mission, are any changes in managers called for?

Again, if you as the client have done thorough and rigorous thinking about all the relevant issues, such changes are unlikely to be made. Experience shows that the best decision often is the "counterintuitive" decision: Assign *more* money to the manager who has been recently "*under*performing" because the well-chosen manager will probably be underperforming only because his or her style is temporarily out of favor and probably will *out*perform when market conditions are more favorable to his or her style.

After a sound investment policy has been formulated and implemented, changes should be made carefully and infrequently.

If this three-tier approach is taken, your decisions will match these tiers, but in *reverse* order:

- Should a manager be changed? The normal expectation is "no." If any manager is identified as "up for review," there should be a rigorous review of the cases for and against action. Clients drop managers they should keep and switch to managers who have just finished their best periods, and the transaction costs of making these changes are high.

First, *never* terminate a manager solely for below-market performance over a one-, two-, or even three-year period. You know from personal experience at ticket counters and tellers' windows that it does not pay to switch from one line to another. Switching investment managers is even less productive. A manager whose record for the recent *past* looks the best seldom does the best in the *following* period. If he or she had an ideal environment in the recent past, the near future very likely will be less hospitable.

Wise investors choose managers very carefully and then stay the course. Very wise and very well-informed investors go one step farther: Having selected a small group of long-term "finalists," they pick the manager whose recent results were depressed by an adverse market environment and get an extra lift from a subsequently more favorable market environment by riding the regression to the mean.

Note that "bad performance" is *any* substantial deviation from expectations, whether above or below. If none are identified, discussion will be concentrated on . . .

- Should the amounts assigned to specific managers be changed (for example, shifting assets *from* managers who have had favorable environments for their type of investing *to* managers whose style of investing has been "difficult")? If such actions *are* proposed (which they should be as seldom as possible), provide the cases for and against each specific action. If none are proposed, discussion will concentrate on . . .

- Should the long-term policy on asset mix be changed? If not, would a significant "temporary" deviation be appropriate? If not, the work of the client is over and the formal part of the meeting is over too.

In this format, decisions are on an "exception" basis and decisions to act are few and far between because you have "done the homework" rigorously and thus have decided on long-term policy *and* on determination of specific missions for managers *and* on specific managers (and so you would make few, if any, changes on any of these fronts).

How long should an ideal meeting on action decisions take? About five minutes—with *no* actions taken because none are needed. As every experienced manager of continuous-process factories knows, one indication of a well-run continuous-process endeavor such as investment management is that "nothing interesting is going on," because anything interesting is a *problem* and a well-run plant is problem-free. It does not need corrections.

The most important contribution you can make to a successful relationship with an investment manager is to select the right manager to begin with. Of course, the first step in selecting the right manager is to know what investment mission the chosen manager will be expected to fulfill.

Prospective investment managers should be examined in three major areas: professional investment competence, commitment to client service, and soundness of business strategy. Of the three areas, professional investment competence is properly given the greatest attention.

A prospective investment management firm should have a clear concept of how it will add value in managing the client's portfolio. That concept can be based on the manager's perception of an *opportunity*—or a problem—in the market that presents favorable opportunities for this particular firm to increase the portfolio's rate of return.

In addition to a cogent concept of how to add value, the investment manager should have developed a sensible process for making decisions to *implement* that concept and should have a valid record of achievement of the results intended by his process to fulfill his concept.

Keep notes on the answers your investment manager gives to your questions. They can be brief but must be saved for future use in comparing the answers you get at other times to the same or similar questions. This simple technique has been used for years—perhaps even for centuries—by the managers of the Scottish investment trusts and by the Japanese.

If and when you decide to terminate an investment manager, do yourself a favor and recognize explicitly that the failure is not the manager's: It is yours. And don't just go looking for a new manager to replace the reject, at least not until you've taken the time and care to learn how you could do a better job of selecting and working with your managers. Chances are, you did not define with rigor the mission for which the manager was hired, you were not as diligent as you should have been in determining the manager's ability to complete the mission successfully, or you did not communicate to the manger all you could have about your aspirations and expectations. (If you *did* do all this, you are a very unusual client.)

Since you start with an "easy answer"—using index funds—be sure the decision to look for *and* pay for an active manager is the right decision for you to be making.

Selecting superior investment managers is *hard.* Investment consulting firms that have specialized for many years in this work—and have large research staffs poring over all the managers' records and asking them all sorts of questions—are typically *not* successful. The managers they select—after all their care and diligence—do not, on average, outperform the market averages.

If you decide you are going to select active managers, be sure you recognize the gauntlet you will be running and the difficult decisions you'll need to make correctly:

- Which managers will outperform the market for many years into the future?

- Can you identify the future's favored few today?

- Will you make the right decisions and take action at the right time?

- If you do select a superior manager, will that manager stay superior, or will the assets managed grow so much, the manager's organization change so much, or the manager's "life situation" change so much that the manager will no longer be able to produce superior results?

- If the manager's investment performance *appears* to be "disappoint-ing," will you be able to tell whether it's just temporary or is the early period in a series of future disappointments?

If you, however reluctantly, resolve to terminate this manager, you'll have to move on to the next section of the gauntlet and face the same diffi-cult decisions all over again.

Changing investment manages is not only difficult to do well, it's expensive. It costs about 4 percent of your assets in transaction costs and market impact costs to switch from one manager to another. And there is another kind of cost: If you accept the idea that changing investment man-agers is a normal part of life, chances are, you'll select managers less care-fully and work with your managers less carefully. In that case you'll be "part of the problem, not part of the solution," and will need to keep chang-ing managers who were not hired with sufficient care. It's a self-destructive cycle; don't get caught up in it.

The concept of using multiple managers has become increasingly pop-ular among large clients in recent years. Several reasons are given:

1. As the client, you can select specialist managers skilled in each of the several different kinds of investing wanted.

2. Clients can diversify against the risk of one manager's investment concept being out of tune with the overall market (as will surely happen from time to time).

3. Managers who fail to perform can be terminated more easily when they manage only part of your funds.

The problem with multiple managers is that the positive reasons become increasingly ephemeral as the number of managers increases. While it may be feasible to select one or two superior managers in a partic-ular specialty, it's harder to pick three or five or seven. There just aren't that many truly superior managers around.

Although diversification does increase with each additional manager, when the separately managed portfolios are amalgamated into one fund and analyzed, it becomes clear that each additional manager adds less and less incremental diversification but does incur higher and higher operating costs and fees—and moves closer and closer to the investment characteris-tics of the market index.

Since index funds are readily available at low cost, the use of different managers cannot be justified as a way to reduce risk, because that can be accomplished more easily and cheaply with a broad market fund.

Rationally, if you are prepared to pay the higher fees inherent in multiple management, the objective must be to increase returns by finding managers who can find and exploit the occasional but significant opportunities that may arise from the mispricing errors of other managers.

Realistically, important opportunities of this kind are found only infrequently. Therefore, the client might well force the manager to place all her bets on a very small number of decisions she believes are most attractive. If this forcing is not done, a client with multiple managers almost certainly will be overpaying for excess diversification. Individual investors who do not wish to place all their assets in index funds might do well, then, to place their remaining assets in funds run by active managers who focus their holdings in relatively few stocks.

The argument that managers can be more easily terminated—with less harm to the fund and less harm to the management firm—if the account is relatively small for both parties is, of course, true, but it may be pernicious. Clients understandably may be less careful in selecting or supervising managers they know they can terminate. And managers may be too cautious in asserting their best investment judgment if these clients may, during an interim period of adverse "performance," terminate them. Most investment managers believe, rightly or wrongly, that the tolerance of their clients for current performance that differs significantly from the market—and for portfolio decisions that differ from the conventional—is *least* when needed most.

Consequently, unless they are guided by clearly defined investment objectives and policies, investment managers may be tempted to act as though their real goal were not to maximize investment results for their clients but to maximize their probability of keeping the account. This could and does result in most portfolios "hugging the index" or "closet indexing" and being stuck in the "muddle of the middle," producing a high-cost but imperfect market portfolio.[2]

If they decide to use active managers, good clients will insist that their managers adhere to the discipline of following through on the agreed-upon investment policy. In other words, as the investor client you will be equally justified and reasonable in terminating a manager for out-of-control results *above* the market as for terminating a manager for out-of-control results *below* the market. Staying with a manager who is not conforming his or her portfolio performance to prior promises is *speculation,* and ultimately you will be "punished."

---

[2]Indeed, roughly 85 percent of the returns of the typical large-stock mutual fund can be explained simply by movements of the Standard & Poor's 500 stock market average.

But staying with a competent investment manager who is conforming to his or her own promises—*particularly* when he or she is out of phase with the current market environment—shows real "client prudence" in investing and ultimately will be rewarded.[3] Only start what you are determined to finish—and then stay the course.

Rare is the manager who achieves long-term results that are substantially superior *after* adjustment for risk. The data are as grim as a photograph of the 1913 graduating class of St. Cyr destined for combat in the trenches of World War I. Over the past 50 years mutual funds in the aggregate have lost 180 basis points compounded annually to the S&P 500, returning 11.8 percent versus 13.6 percent for the benchmark index.[4] Over the past decade, S&P 500 returns have been better than the results of 89 percent of all U.S. mutual funds. The average *under*performance of mutual funds is reported to be 340 basis points.[5] That's why investors find it distressingly difficult to find managers who can and will achieve consistently superior results. It's also why experience teaches that reaching for "the best" manager so frequently produces real disappointment for investors. Like Icarus, trying too hard can lead to serious harm. Switching around among mutual funds is what causes the average mutual fund investor to obtain long-term returns that produce a distressing *one-third less* than the average mutual fund. This serious slippage is the self-inflicted pain caused by those who do not or cannot appreciate the importance of fidelity.

[3]As I know from experience. In the mid-1970s I increased my commitment to John Neff's Gemini Fund—a lot. I knew John well enough to know that he was very careful to control and limit risk. The stock market had been very negative on the "value" stocks John liked to own. Conventional investors were not discriminating carefully between real risk and perception, but John clearly would. As a duo-fund, Gemini's Capital shares had experienced the leveraged impact of a several-year decline in the value area of the stock market and were selling at a discount from net asset value. I calculated how much broker's margin could be used without getting a margin call—even after a 20 percent further drop in stock prices— and bought in, fully margined. As the market rose, I enjoyed the "six layered" benefits of John Neff as my investment manager, plus the recovery of the market, plus the superior returns to "value" stocks, plus the shift from "discount" to "premium" in the Gemini Capital shares, plus the leverage of the duo-fund, plus the leverage of heavy margin. Despite all the apparent leverage risk, I felt very confident—and quite safe—because I knew John was both rigorously risk-averse and a disciplined, rational investor. The following 20 years (thanks to John's great work as "the professional investor's favorite investment professional") were very well rewarded—with minimal risk.

[4]John C. Bogle, "The Clash of Cultures in Investing: Complexity versus Simplicity." Speech given at the Money Show, Orlando, Florida, February 3, 1999.

[5]"Strategy: The Global Going Gets Tough." *The Competitive Edge,* Morgan Stanley Dean Witter, February 8, 1999. The "professional shortfall" is found in international markets as well.

While most investors take investment services as they are offered—in a conventionally blended form—it is possible to unbundle services into separate levels. There are five levels of decisions for each investor to make:

Level 1: Asset mix—the optimal proportion of equities, bonds, private equity, and so forth, for the "policy normal" of the investor's portfolio.

Level 2: Equity mix—"policy normal" proportions in various types of stocks: growth versus value, large cap versus small cap, domestic versus international. The same decisions are made on subcategories for each major asset class.

Level 3: Active versus passive management—the appropriate method chosen for implementation of the "policy normal" mix of investments.

Level 4: Specific manager selection (where most investors and investment committees unfortunately concentrate their time and effort)—deciding which investment firms will manage each component of the overall portfolio, firing the most disappointing and hiring the most promising.

Level 5: Active portfolio management—changing portfolio strategy, selecting securities, and executing transactions.

The least costly *and* the most valuable service is on level 1: getting it basically right on long-term goals and the asset mix—often helped by wise investment counseling. The last two levels—the active management of managers (through hiring and firing) and the active management of portfolios (through buying and selling)—are the most expensive and the least likely to add value. The results are most likely to be particularly grim when the individual investor decides to do the buying and selling himself or herself. (Remember, the taxes as well as the operating costs are much higher with all this activity.)

At level 1—setting realistic long-term investment objectives—*every* investor can be a winner. However, as the evidence makes increasingly clear, very few can or will win in the increasingly hyperactive and counterproductive pursuit of comparative advantage on level 5.

That's the ultimate irony of the Loser's Game: We can be, and all too often are, dazzled by the excitement and the action and the "chance to win" on level 5—Mr. Market's favorite territory—where the costs to play are so high and the rewards are so small. Even worse, the search for ways to beat the market distracts us from focusing on level 1, where the costs are low and the rewards can be large.

Sustaining a long-term focus at either market highs or market lows is notoriously hard to do. In either case, emotions are strongest and current market action appears most demanding of change because the apparent "facts" seem most compelling at market highs and market lows. This is why investors can benefit so much from sound investment counseling on levels 1, 2, and 3.

Professional executives who are responsible for pension and endowment funds—often advised by experienced consultants with massive databases and numerous staff researchers who diligently monitor managers—have this set of experiences: The managers they *hire* tend to underperform the managers they *fired* and replaced. Take extra time and care to select the manager you would be ready to "double up" with whenever recent performance is significantly below the market averages.

The beginning of wisdom is to understand that few—if any—major investment organizations will outperform the market over long periods of time and that it is very difficult to estimate which managers will outperform it. The next step is to decide whether—even if it could be won—this loser's game is worth playing.

Finally, a word on fees. Investment management fees usually are set by the managers and usually are *not* negotiable. However, you can take your business elsewhere. Be sure of your beliefs about investment management fees. Here are some points to consider. Fees have been going up over the years even though a majority of managers do not keep up with the market averages. Conventionally, management fees are presented as a percentage of assets and are "only" ½ percent of assets or less. But wait. Should clients pay fees as a percentage of assets *or* as a percentage of returns—or, even better, as a percentage of incremental returns achieved over and above the market's return, risk-adjusted? If you think that the rational level of fees is in proportion to the benefit the client gets, you'll be impressed to learn that the fees most managers charge—relative to incremental risk-adjusted returns—are *over* 100 percent. That's worth thinking about.

C H A P T E R

16

ESTIMATING THE MARKET— ROUGHLY

I NVESTORS NATURALLY WANT TO KNOW the most probable investment outlook for the years ahead.[1] Long-term investors understand
from experience the remarkable pattern—and discipline—of the
bell curve of economic behavior and the central tendency of the
major forces in the economy and the stock market to move toward
the mean or "normal." Long-term investors understand that the farther away
current events are from the mean at the center of the bell curve, the stronger
the forces of mean reversion become, unrelentingly pulling the current data
toward the center and normal.

One good way to be realistic about future returns is to assume that the
future range of price/earnings multiples and profits will be within their
historical upper and lower limits and will appear with increasing frequency at values closer and closer to the mean. (Caution: If the market has
been going up, investors—who usually evaluate future prospects by looking into the *rear*view mirror—may add some upward momentum; if the mar-

---

[1]Understanding the outlook for the next days or weeks is easy. As J. P. Morgan said, "It will
fluctuate."

ket has been trending down, they may add some downward momentum—temporarily.)

While the economy is extraordinarily complex at a detailed level—and the stock market reflects all sorts of factors in every domestic and global industry, in thousands of companies, *and* in the overall economy—two big factors determine the dominant reality for investors: corporate profits (and the dividends they provide) and the rate at which these earnings are capitalized—the price/earnings ratio (determined by interest rates[2] plus or minus a "speculative" factor reflecting how optimistic or pessimistic investors currently feel).

To start, if dividends yield 1½ percent and corporate earnings grow at 4½ percent—the middle of their normal range of growth over the long term, which has been 4 to 5 percent—then a composite of 6 percent is the reasonable first part of the "fundamental" rate of return to expect. Next, because securities are marketable, what change in valuation is reasonable? As the starting point, the average price/earnings ratio in recent decades has been 15.5×. If you believe the economy is now a fundamentally stronger environment for corporations, you *might* boost that to 17 to 18 times earnings or *maybe* even to 20 times.

Historical perspective is always helpful.[3] How do these two major factors—earnings and P/E—explain America's best-ever bull market in 1982–1999? Here's how: First, corporate profits in 1982 were only 3.5 percent of gross domestic product, significantly *below* the 4 to 6 percent normal range. By the late 1990s corporate profits were almost 6 percent, the *high* side of the normal range. That's a big change. Next, interest rates on long-term U.S. government bonds plunged over that period from 14 percent to 5 percent. (This single change would multiply the market value of those bonds *eight*fold, or 13 percent compounded annually.) As with all long-term changes in the market's valuation, the main forces were fundamental and *objective.* Also included was an additional *subjective* factor that depends on how investors *feel:* very pessimistic in 1974 but very optimistic in 1999. Over the same years, partly as a result of earnings growth but primarily because of that major decline in interest rates—because expectations for inflation had fallen so substantially—the Dow Jones Industrial

---

[2]Reflecting expected inflation.

[3]*Fortune,* November 22, 1999. *Irrational Exuberance,* Robert Shiller's eloquent and fact-founded review of the U.S. stockmarket at the height of the new economy euphoria, is a superb example of a rational appraisal. (Princeton University Press, 2000).

Average (with all dividends reinvested) increased nearly *20* times for a compounded annual return of 19 percent.

In cheerful disregard of the great powers driving regression to the mean, investors almost always project the past market and economic behavior into the future, somehow expecting more of the same. In the early 1970s investors were sure that inflation would stay very high and earnings would stay very low or get even worse, and most newspapers and magazines featured the same grim and grizzly prospects. In 2000 investors were remarkably (but almost predictably) highly optimistic and anticipated more of the same compounding—particularly those who were enamored of Internet stocks and were chanting the mantra of all stock market bubbles[4]: "This time it's different."

Jack Bogle, as usual, has a clear and straightforward approach. First, divide investment returns into the fundamental return and the speculative return. Fundamental return is the combination of current dividends and the annual growth in earnings. Speculative return is the change—plus *or* minus—in evaluation relative to earnings: the price/earnings ratio. History can tell us a lot, and those who do not study history and learn from it are doomed to repeat it. First, remember that the Dow Jones Industrial Average was 1000 in 1968 *and* in 1982. At year end 1964 *and* year end 1981 the Dow was 875—17 long years with zero net change because even though corporate profits were up a lot, interest rates had soared from 4 percent to 15 percent, which compressed the price/earnings multiple substantially, *and* investors had "learned" to be deeply pessimistic. From that low level, where did the market go?

In 1988, dividends yielded 3.5 percent, and over the next 11 years earnings grew at 7.1 percent annually. Good news for investors: The fundamental return—dividends plus earnings growth—was 10.6 percent per annum. But that's not all: Investors got paid a lot more. While the fundamental return was 10.6 percent, the total investment return was a stunning 18.9 percent. The difference was made up by the add-on of 8.3 percent in speculative return as the price/earnings ratio took flight and more than doubled from 12× to 29×! Could it last? Of course not. Regression to the mean was sure to come again. Just as a price/earnings multiple of 12 was too low— and long-term investors were eventually certain to get a strong lift from "mean regression"—a price/earnings multiple of 29 was too high and eventually was sure to go down.

---

[4]Other investor enthusiasms were canals in Britain in the 1830s, railroads in Europe and America in the 1850s, automobiles in the 1920s, and real estate in Japan in the 1980s.

Here's another way to estimate likely future returns.[5] Stock returns always add up to the sum of the current dividend yield, plus dividends/earnings per share growth plus or minus any change in the valuation of dividends/earnings per share. Historically, the sum of these three components has worked out to something like this: 3.5 percent + 2 percent + 2 percent = 7.5 percent in real terms. Today we start with a dividend yield of 1.5 percent. Assume future long-term real dividends/earnings per share growth to be an optimistic 2.5 percent. Realistically, we can no longer count on rising price/earnings multiples. Therefore, the stock return arithmetic works out to 1.5 percent + 2.5 percent + 0 percent = 4 percent. You can change any of the factors as you see fit, but use the lessons and patterns of history and always strive to be rational.

Another way to make an estimate of the future is to assume that we are in the middle of a very long-term period and that the real—after adjusting for inflation—rate of return over the whole period will be the historically normal 6.75 percent. Since the returns of the past 20 years were 13.3 percent, then to average 8.75 percent, the *next* 20 years will return only 0.6 percent. And if the long-term average will be 9 percent, the next 20 years can be expected to return 4.9 percent.[6]

The possibility of such outcomes should not be dismissed out of hand—and certainly not because the stock market has generated excellent returns in the *past* 20 years. For the period 1901–1921 the real average annual return of the U.S. stock market was 0.2 percent. For the period 1929–1949 it was 0.4 percent, and for the period 1966–1986 it was 1.9 percent. In other words, for periods covering more than 60 percent of the twentieth century, the real annual returns generated by the third best performing stock market in the world were less than 2.0 percent.

Ben Graham wisely cautioned in the introduction to his textbook *Security Analysis:* "Long-term investors must be careful not to learn too much from recent experience." He was talking about the 1929 market crash and the ghastly months and years that followed. He could just as easily have been talking about the Internet market or any of a long series of times when all or part of the stock market overreacted to recent events, sometimes positively and sometimes negatively.

Estimating the stock market *roughly* is not hard, but estimating it accurately is truly impossible. Equally, estimating approximately where the stock market will normally be in the long run is not hard, but estimating

[5]Canadian market observer Keith Ambachtsheer articulates this approach.

[6]Cambridge Associates promulgates this perspective.

how it will move over the next few months is nearly impossible—and point-less. Remember that over many, many years the major components that determine the level of the stock market have remarkably consistent patterns of behavior *and* a powerful tendency for regression to the mean or the nor-mal condition, particularly in the long run.

The main reason for estimating the current level of the market and its probable direction is entirely defensive and is done mostly to protect our-selves from ourselves and our all-too-human tendencies to get caught by Mr. Market in the same excessive optimism or pessimism that can infect "the crowd."

17

THE INDIVIDUAL INVESTOR

INDIVIDUAL INVESTORS ARE profoundly different from institutional investors. It's not just that individual investors have less money. One difference is decisive: Each individual is mortal. Inevitable mortality is a dominant reality for all individual investors—as individuals and as investors.

Life *is* short. Those of us who are earning incomes usually have a finite period of years in which to build our lifetime savings and investments. And those who are no longer earning and saving have finite financial resources on which they will depend for the indefinite duration of their lives.

Another way in which individual investors are different is that their money often takes on great symbolic meaning and can engage their emotions powerfully. The key to success in investing is *rationality*. However, most investors can't help letting their emotions get involved and at central junctions even get the upper hand. Many investors feel that their money represents themselves and the "worth" of their lives (as entrepreneurs often identify their value and their self-worth with their companies.) This "my money is me" syndrome is particularly common and virulent among elderly people. If it happens to someone in your family, be tolerant: It's just a way of "expressing" one's fear of death.

Yet another important difference is that individual investors have considerable power to affect others—both financially and emotionally—with gifts and bequests made or not made or made larger or smaller than antici-pated or considered "fair." The emotional power and symbolism of money are often more important than its economic power, and individual investors will be wise to deal carefully with both.

All investors share one formidable and all too easily underestimated adversary: inflation. This adversary is particularly dangerous for individual investors.

For individual investors, over the long run inflation is *the* major prob-lem, not the attention-getting daily or cyclical changes in securities prices that most investors fret about. The corrosive power of inflation is truly daunting: At 3 percent inflation, the purchasing power of your money is cut in half in 24 years (see Figure 17–1). At 5 percent inflation, the pur-chasing power of your money is cut in half in less than 15 years—and cut in half again in the *next* 15 years. At 7 percent, your purchasing power drops to just one-quarter of its present level in 21 years—the elapsed time between retirement at 65 and retirement at age 86, an increasingly normal life expectancy. This is clearly serious business, particularly when you are retired and have no way to add capital to offset the dreadful erosion of pur-chasing power caused by inflation.

For individual investors, inflation is the major problem.

Individual investors are also differentiated from institutional investors by the fact that each of us has responsibilities we take very personally: edu-cating our children, providing security for ourselves and our loved ones, helping to pay for health care for elderly relatives, contributing to the schools and other institutions from which we have benefited or hope our

FIGURE 17-1   Effect of increasing inflation on purchasing power.

Rate of Inflation (%)	Time to Cut Your Money in Half (Years)
2	24
3	18
4	14
5	12
6	11

communities will benefit, and so forth. In addition, as individual investors, each of us wants to provide a strong self-defense against catastrophe, including the risk of living longer and needing more health care than anticipated. Finally, most individuals wish to leave something to their children or grandchildren to enhance their lives. (Our children having better lives is, for most people, the real meaning of progress.) Not only are these responsibilities taken very personally, in many cases the amounts that will be involved are unknown and may become almost "unlimited." The potential cost of health care in old age is an uncomfortable example.

Most individual investors have a long-term implicit "balance sheet" of assets and responsibilities. However, most investors have not examined their own total financial picture or put it all down on paper. And most have not been explicit about the direct and indirect stakeholders—the "we"—in their balance sheet responsibilities.

In planning the "responsibility" side of your investor's balance sheet, you will want to decide who is included in your "we" and for what purpose. How much responsibility do you plan to take for your children's education? College is costly. Graduate school is increasingly accepted as the norm, and it's costly too. After providing for education, is helping with a child's first home important to you? Help in starting a business or a dental practice? How about your parents, brothers, and sisters or your in-laws? Under what circumstances would they need your financial help? How much might be involved and when? Be sure you know what your total commitments would add up to and when the money would be needed.

Saving naturally and necessarily comes before investing because we can invest only what we have saved. Saving has one special characteristic: You can decide what you want done, and you can *make* it happen! Buying straw hats in the fall or Christmas cards in January and saving through the many other daily forms of conscientious underspending can make a splendid difference over the years, particularly when it is matched with a sensible long-term approach to investing.

The first purpose of saving is to accumulate a defensive reserve that can be turned to for help—like a fire extinguisher—if and when trouble comes. And like a fire extinguisher, such a reserve should be used boldly and fully whenever needed. After providing for protection against serious contingencies, further savings can be invested for the long term.

One of the core concepts and basic themes of this book is that funds available for long-term investment will do best for the investor if they are invested in stocks and *kept* in stocks over time. But what about elderly investors whose life expectancy is less than the 10 years that approximates "long term?" Shouldn't they, the conventional wisdom would have it, invest primarily in bonds to "preserve capital?" As usual, the conventional wisdom may be wrong.

While retired investors may decide for "peace of mind" that they prefer to invest in relatively stable securities with relatively high income, they should know that they are letting their emotional interests dominate their economic interests. They may well be right to do so, but not necessarily. For individuals, as for institutions, investing in bonds to generate more current income dooms the individual to Ellis's law: $1 of extra income costs $1.50 in the total return forgone by not investing as much in long-term equity investments. This may be a heavy price to pay for the apparent conservatism of shifting assets into higher-yielding "defensive" investments such as bonds and income stocks *and* becoming a stationary target for inflation to do its eroding harm.

Moreover, while an elderly invest*or* may not expect to live for long, the invest*ments*—after being inherited by the beneficiaries—may have a very long-term mission. There may be no reason to limit the time horizon of the investments to the owner's lifetime when the owner's true objectives—providing for children, spouse, or alma mater—have a much longer-term horizon.[1]

If you use your defensive reserve cautiously or only partially, you will simply require a proportionately larger reserve—and it's costly (in opportunity costs) to have a larger reserve than is really needed. The reserve is on hand to be *spent,* not to be held back in time of need. To be a truly successful lifetime investor, the first and central challenge is to "know thyself"—understand your personal financial goals and what would truly be successful for *you.* As "Adam Smith" (George G. W. Goodman) wisely counseled: "If you don't know who you are, the stock market is an expensive place to find out!" (So are the markets for real estate, commodities, and options.)

Investors will be wise to take time to learn as much as possible about themselves—and how they will feel and behave as investors. For example, here's a simple test—with a friendly twist—that for most investors provides useful insight.

Question: If you had your choice, which would you prefer?

Choice A: Stocks go *up* by quite a lot and *stay up* for many years.

Choice B: Stocks go *down* by quite a lot and *stay down* for many
years.

---

[1]Besides, one of the secrets to a long and happy life is to "keep climbing" and stay, in Disraeli's felicitous phrase, "in league with the future." It keeps us young to invest in stocks.

Without looking ahead, which did you choose? If you selected choice A, you would be joining 90 percent of the professional investors who've taken this test. Comforting to know most pros are with you? Shouldn't be. Here's why. Unless you are a long-term *seller* of stocks, you would have chosen *against* your own interests if you chose A.

First, remember that when you buy a common stock, what you really buy is the right to receive the dividends paid on that share of stock.[2] Just as we buy cows for their milk and hens for their eggs, we buy stocks for their current and future dividends. If you ran a dairy, wouldn't you prefer to have cow prices low when you were buying so that you could get more gallons of milk for your investment in cows?

The lower the price of the shares are when you buy, the more shares you will get for every $1,000 you invest and the greater the amount of dollars you will receive in dividends on your investment. Therefore, if you are a saver and a *buyer* of shares—as most investors are and will continue to be for many years—your real long-term interest is, curiously, to have stock prices go *down* quite a lot and stay there so you can accumulate more shares at lower prices and therefore receive more dividends with the savings you invest.

Thus, the right long-term choice is the counterintuitive choice B. It's best for you to have stock prices go way *down* and stay down so that you can acquire more rights to receive more dividends in future years with the money you invest now.

This has been much more than a clever explanation of a question with a twist. It can be the key insight that will enable you to enjoy greater success as an investor *and* greater peace of mind during your investing career.

Most investors, being all too human, much prefer stock markets that *have been* rising and feel most enthusiastic about buying more shares when stock prices are already high, causing the future rate of return from their dividends to be axiomatically low. (The dollars of dividends to be received will be the same per share of stock whether you pay a lot or a little for the shares.) Similarly, most investors feel quite negatively about stocks *after* share prices have gone down and are most tempted to sell out at the wrong

---

[2] Yes, you also get the right to vote on the selection of auditors, the election of directors, and so forth. And you get the right to be bought out at a higher price if and when there's a future takeover. But realistically, very few votes of shareholders go against management's recommendations and unanticipated buyouts occur at very few companies, and so these shareholder rights are usually not very important compared with dividends. Yes, you also get the right to sell the stock to another investor, hopefully, of course, at a higher price. But what determines the price the next investor will gladly pay? The present value of expected future dividends.

FIGURE 17-2   **This chart shows how important reinvesting dividends has been, even in two long periods when stocks achieved virtually no appreciation: the 25 years from 1930 to 1955 and the 20 years from 1965 to 1985. As shown in the chart, $1.00 grew to $105.96 as a result of price appreciation, with no dividends reinvested, but that $1.00 grew to become $2,591.79 with dividends reinvested.**

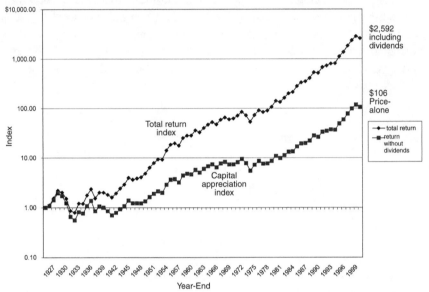

time—when prices are already low—and the future dividend yield on the price paid will be high (see Figure 17-2).

If you can use the insight from our simple quiz and incorporate the *rational* answer into your investment thinking and *behavior,* you will appreciate that your human emotions often move contrary to your rational economic interests. You will school yourself to go against the crowd *and your own feelings* and will strive to avoid the temptation to jump on the bandwagon to buy when stocks are high or jump off when stocks are low.

As a long-term investor, you want to see stocks lower.

Don't confuse facts with feelings. Strive to be consistently rational. Another all-too-human characteristic of most investors is paying too close attention to the day-to-day and even hour-to-hour ups and downs of stock prices. Rationally, we know that most of the changes in share prices are "noise" or almost random fluctuations. Consider the data: Most stocks will change by 4 percent or more between the high and low prices during each trading day. There are nearly 250 trading days a year, which would imply a total change in prices over the year of 1,000 percent (4 percent × 250 days). However, the price of most stocks changes less than 15 percent net over a year, and so more than 98 percent of the gross change is just flutter or noise. Investors should ignore the dance of stock prices, fascinating and seductive as the activity of Mr. Market may be.

Of course, investors must live with disconcerting price fluctuations in securities prices, just as the parents of teenagers must learn to live with a teenager's disruptive remarks and challenging behavior.

In my first year on Wall Street I was in a "training" program with a group of "freshly minted" MBAs. We all looked forward to our final session: a meeting with the senior partner, a patrician man who had amassed a large personal fortune through astute investments over many years. Asked about his secret for success and what he would advise young men like us to do, he took a long, thoughtful pause and then summarized his accumulated experience in this blunt maxim: "Don't lose!"

When I first heard this advice 40 years ago, it seemed far too simple, but as the years have gone by, I've become convinced that it is very sound. Don't set yourself up for serious, irrevocable losses. Naturally, you can't invest without absorbing lots of small interim losses. Markets do fluctuate, and nothing ventured, nothing gained. But don't take untoward risks. Don't swing for the fences. Don't invest with borrowed money. As mentioned earlier, there are old pilots and there are bold pilots, but there are no old, bold pilots.

If you find yourself getting caught up in the excitement of a rising market or distressed by a falling market, stop. Break it off. Go for a walk and cool down. Otherwise, you will soon become part of the "crowd," wanting to *do* something—and you will start making errors, perhaps grave errors that you will regret. Benign neglect is, for most investors, the secret to long-term success in investing.

Individuals with large fortunes—$25 million and over—can obtain good investment counsel as a "separate account." Those with less than $2 million usually cannot. Their accounts are simply too small to be important to a first-rate investment manager. Fortunately, all investors do have an alternative: mutual funds. Two types of funds have particular interest. One type is an index fund, run at low costs and fees and designed to replicate any one of several recognized market indexes, such as the Standard & Poor's 500 and the Russell 2000[3] (see Chapter 4).

[3]Vanguard offers a series of such funds.

Closed-end mutual funds are another type that is interesting, specifically those now selling at a discount *and* obliged by their pride or bylaws to become open-end funds—which would eliminate the discount—within a reasonable time period. Such funds are particularly interesting if their long-term style of investing—"growth" or "value"—is currently out of favor and you can buy into them during their "off season."

As with institutional investing, individuals who have a separate account will be wise to agree *in writing* with the investment manager on the overall program by which their funds will be invested: long-term objectives, investment policy constraints, and performance expectations in various market environments. Individuals who invest in mutual funds can do nearly as much by reading carefully the written statement in each fund's prospectus of its long-term objectives, policies, and performance expectations.

You can increase your chances of achieving superior investment performance—which means *reliably achieving your own explicit and realistic investment objectives*—by taking the time once a year for a formal review of your investment objectives, financial resources, financial responsibilities, and recent investment results compared with prior realistic expectations.

Although the focus of attention typically will be on investments, the following should also be examined: savings, insurance, bank credit available, current debts, probable obligations to help or support others in your "we" group, annual income versus expenditure, and estate plans. The objective of this disciplined exercise is to "turn on the lights" and look over the whole situation.

If you have successfully saved and invested enough to have ample funds for all chosen responsibilities or obligations, you have truly *won* the "money game." Bravo! This is an appropriately thrilling achievement. Winners should be careful never to put their victory back at risk, particularly through unnecessary or injudicious borrowing or by committing too much to any single investment or overextending responsibilities and commitments.

Winners should avoid speculations in an attempt to win *big*. It's not worth the risk of losing enough to become a "nonwinner"—not just a loser but truly a sucker. Winners should also be careful about being "too careful," as was noted above; a shift to nominally "conservative" investing can leave investments exposed—and at risk—to the erosion of inflation. Nathan Mayer Rothschild, the founder of that family's great fortune, explained what it takes: "It requires a great deal of boldness and a great deal of caution to make a great fortune; and when you have got it, it requires ten times as much wit to keep it."

As an individual investor, these 10 "commandments" may be useful guides to thinking about your decisions on investments:

1. Don't speculate. If you must "play the market" to satisfy an emotional "itch," recognize that you are gambling on your ability to beat the pros and limit the amounts you play with to those you would gamble with the pros at Las Vegas. (Keep accurate records of your results, and you'll soon persuade yourself to quit!)

2. Save.

3. Don't do anything in investing primarily for "tax reasons." Tax shelters are poor investments. Tax loss selling is primarily a way for brokers to increase their commissions.

    There are exceptions, of course, and some are important. Be sure you have an astute estate plan that is current with your financial situation and the ever-changing tax laws. Give careful consideration to the "secret" benefit of index fund investing: *low taxes.* Because portfolio turnover is so low, taxes on gains—particularly short-term gains—are much lower than taxes on the typical "active" mutual funds. The reduction in taxes is currently averaging over 3 percent in annual benefit to investors.

    There are two more exceptions. Making charitable gifts with low-cost stock can make sense *if* you were going to sell the stock anyway. Set up an IRA if you can and maximize contributions to your 401(k) or profit-sharing plan every year.

"It requires a great deal of boldness and a great deal of caution to make a great fortune."

4. Don't think of your home as an investment. Think of it as a place to live with your family, period. Over the past 25 years home prices have risen less than the consumer price index and have returned less than Treasury bills.

5. Never do commodities. Consider the experience of a commodities broker who over a decade advised nearly *1,000* customers on commodities. How many made money? Not even one.[4] But the broker did, thanks to commissions.

[4]John Train, *The Money Masters* (New York: Harper & Row, 1987).

6.   Don't be confused about stockbrokers. They are usually very nice people, but their job is not to make money *for* you. Their job is to make money *from* you. While some stockbrokers are wonderfully conscientious people who are devoted to doing a good, thoughtful job for the customers they work with over many, many years, you can't *assume* that your stockbroker is working that way for you. Some do, but most simply can't afford it. (Be realistic: The typical stockbroker "talks to" 200 customers with *total* invested assets of $5 million. To earn $100,000 a year, he needs to generate about $300,000 in gross commissions, or 6 percent of the money he talks to. To generate this volume of commissions, the broker cannot afford the time to learn what is "right." He has to keep the money moving—and it will be *your* money.)

7.   Don't invest in new or "interesting" investments. They are all too often designed to be *sold to* investors, not to be *owned by* investors.[5] (When the novice fisherman expressed wonderment that fish would actually go for the gaudily decorated lures offered at the bait shop, the proprietor's laconic reply was, "We don't sell them lures to fish.")

8.   Don't invest in bonds because you've heard that bonds are conservative or for safety of either income or capital. Bond prices fluctuate nearly as much as stock prices do, and bonds are a poor defense against the real risk of long-term investing: inflation.

9.   Write out your long-term goals, your long-term investing program, *and* your estate plan and stay with them. Review these plans at least once each decade. Annual reviews are recommended. Don't procrastinate.

10.   Don't trust your emotions. When you feel euphoric, you're probably in for a bruising. When you feel down, remember that it's dark-

---

[5]My Aunt Saizie is in her late eighties. After years and years of careful saving and wise investing, she built up a portfolio of common stocks worth nearly $100,000. She asked me whether she should take the strong recommendation of a very nice-looking young man from the local broker's office. His proposition didn't sound quite right to her: sell all her stocks (incurring a large capital gain) and put most of the money in Treasury bills for safety of principal and then use the rest to buy stock options so that she could participate in any bull market that might come along. Fortunately, Saizie is too wise and shrewd an investor to get drawn in by something that "interesting." (Imagine all the commissions that would have been generated for the broker!)

est just before dawn and take no action. Activity in investing is almost always in surplus.

Finally, a special word to those who participate in a 401(k) plan—or any other Defined Contribution plan—over which you, as a participant have "investment discretion." Concentrate your investments in index funds.

Do not invest a lot in your own company—wonderful as the company may be—because depending on your job at one company is already a major "total economic portfolio" concentration. Your retirement fund should be "safety first" and safety means *defense.* If you have any doubts, read all about Lucent and Enron—two of numerous great American companies that later lost 90 percent of their market value and were forced to lay off large numbers of loyal workers: savings lost, job lost, and dream lost.

CHAPTER 18

PLANNING
YOUR PLAY

YES, DEATH *IS* EVERY INDIVIDUAL'S ultimate reality, but as an *investor,* you may be making too much of it. If, for example, you plan to leave most of your capital in bequests to your children, the appropriate time horizon for your *family* investment policy—even if you are well into your seventies or eighties—may be so long term that you'd be correct to ignore investment conventions such as "Older people should invest in bonds for higher income and greater safety."

This may *sound* okay, but the wiser, better decision for you and your family may be to invest 100 percent in equities because your *investing* horizon is far longer than your *living* horizon. The conventional wisdom—"to determine the percentage of your assets you should have in stocks, subtract your age from 100"—is usually wrong for two main reasons: (1) It compels you to reduce the proportion of stocks and increase the proportion of cash and bonds with each passing year, which you can do only by selling your stocks, generating a costly and unnecessary tax bill for yourself, and (2) if the people you love (your family and heirs) or even the organizations you love (your favorite charities) are likely to outlive you—as they almost certainly will—you should extend your investment planning horizon to cover not just your own life span but theirs as well. If, for instance, you are 40 years old and have a five-year-old son, your real investment horizon is not just another 45 years (your own future life expectancy), but closer to the 80 more years your son will live. Even if you are 75 years old, your investment horizon could be equally long if you have young grandchildren or a favorite charity.

Most investors' actual time horizons for investments are quite *long*—20 years, 30 years, and often 50 years or more—because the investments they pass on to others will continue to be active well past the period of their own lives. We investors *are* mortal, but our investments don't know it—and don't care.

Remember "Adam Smith's" admonition: "The stock doesn't know you own it." This observation applies to *all* investments: stocks, bonds, buildings, and so forth. All have value today and will have a future value irrespective of who owns them. Therefore, investing should always be done for *investment* reasons and not for *personal* reasons such as your chronological age.

Don't change your investments just because you have reached a different age or have retired. If you could afford fine paintings, you wouldn't change the ones you love the most simply because you had reached retirement or had celebrated your seventieth or eightieth birthday. It's the same with investments: Maintain the strategy you have set for yourself if you can afford to do so.

Don't change your investments just because you have come to a different age.

Compounding is powerful. Remember the grateful sultan who offered to reward his wazir generously for a great deed that had saved the sultan's empire? The wazir modestly offered to accept only one grain of wheat on the first square of a checkerboard, only two grains on the next, four grains on the third, eight grains on the fourth, and so on—and on and on. The crafty wazir indicated that he had no need for a great reward and that the symbolism of this compound giving would please his humble, grateful heart. Joyfully, the sultan seized upon this seemingly simple way to clear his obligation, but he did not reckon on the formidable power of compounding. *Any*thing doubled 64 consecutive times will balloon—and balloon again. In the story the few grains of wheat compounded to a total value that was greater than *all* the wealth in the entire empire. To defend his honor before Allah, the sultan ended up turning over the entire empire to the wazir.

Here's a variation that should be more familiar to most people today: If you had invested $100 in shares of common stock at the start of the twentieth century, what would that investment be worth today? Quick answer: $733,383. Wow, $100 grew to nearly three-quarters of a million dollars! But not so fast! Let's ask some clarifying questions.

Question: How much of the 95 years' gain came in the last 20 years?

Answer: Most of it. In fact, by 1975 the fund had increased to only $75,000. The other $643,000 came in the last two decades as the stock market flourished.

Question: How much of the apparently wonderful gain was really just the "pass-through" of inflation?

Answer: Most of it. The *real* gain over the entire century was just over $40,000—certainly a substantial gain on $100 but, just as certainly, only 6 percent of the *nominal* gain of $733,382.

The main message is *not* how wonderfully compounding increases real wealth. The main message is that inflation relentlessly destroys wealth's purchasing power—*almost* as rapidly as economic gains are building wealth. Only the real *net* gain is spendable. Beware of the promotional materials and advertising that are deceiving investors with a Lorelei promise of phenomenal "riches" in the future *without* explaining the grim negative—and simultaneous—impact of inflation.

Inflation is the ruthless, unrelenting destroyer of your capital. To purchase an item costing $100 in 1960 would have cost $500 in 1995. In other words, during just one generation inflation reduced the value of each dollar by 4.8 percent *compounded annually,* which amounts to a withering 80 percent!

Your investments do not know your wishes or intentions—and really don't care.

The grinding, corrosive power of inflation is very clearly and emphatically the investor's worst enemy. In just 20 years, as shown in Figure 18-1, the purchasing power of $1.00 shrank to $0.35.

The power of inflation to impose real harm on investments may be seen by studying the Dow Jones Industrial Average *after* adjustment for inflation. Note particularly:

FIGURE 18-1   The shrinking value of $1.00.

Source: Consumer Price Index, U.S. Department of Labor.

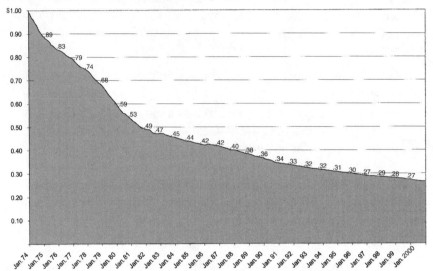

- From 1977 to 1982, the inflation-adjusted Dow Jones Industrial Average went from 270 to 100—a five-year *loss* of 63 percent!

- It's important for rational, long-term investors to know and remember that in the 15 years from the late 1960s to the early 1980s the unweighted stock market *adjusted for inflation* plunged about 80 percent. As a result, the decade of the 1970s was actually worse for investors than was the decade of the 1930s.

- In 1993, the Dow Jones was equal to its inflation-adjusted level in 1928. Sixty-five years was a long, long time to wait to get even.

In developing a sound financial plan investors will want to begin with good answers ("good" because they are both *comforting* and *rational*) to these three overarching questions:

- Does our plan assure me of having enough income to pay for an appropriate standard of living—*after overcoming inflation*—during retirement? For most people, this "sufficiency of income" works out to 75 to 80 percent of preretirement spending *plus* 3 to 4 percent annually *compounded* to offset inflation.

- Will our financial reserves be sufficient to cover unexpected emergencies—usually health crises—particularly in old age? Beware!

Eighty percent of a typical person's lifetime expenditures on health care are spent in the last six months of that person's life.

Women live longer than men, and wives are often younger than their husbands. Therefore, most couples will want to pay particular attention to providing adequately for the wife's years as a widow.

• Will the remaining capital match our goals and intentions for giving to heirs and charities?

If these core questions are not answered fully and affirmatively, your plan needs to be reconsidered and changed—perhaps substantially. Do it now so that you'll have time on your side to work for you as long as possible.

Write down your goals—with the target dates by which you intend to achieve them—so that you can measure your actual progress compared to your explicit plan, because in all matters of investing *time* is key.

Investing is not necessarily best when it is driven by noninvestment events such as the timing of children's admission to college, the receipt of an inheritance, and the date of retirement. Separate *when* you invest from *how* you invest. Your investments do not know your wishes or intentions—and really don't care. As an investor, you must adapt to the market. The market won't adapt to you. If today isn't the right time for you to implement a long-term investment program—because the market appears too high—you can always put your capital in safe storage with a money market fund and then convert to long-term investments when you believe market prices are appropriate or, usually more wisely, invest in steady, equal amounts over a several-year period. (This is called *dollar-cost averaging,* and it has the happy result that your average purchase price will be less than the average price at which you purchase!)

Over your lifetime as an investor, your optimal investment program will change—and change again—partly because your circumstances and resources will change and partly because your objectives and priorities will change. But the more thoughtfully and soundly you plan and the farther in advance you do your planning, the less you will need to change your plan as time passes. Planning a sound long-term investment program is often done best in 10-year chunks of time. This is the case because working with decadelong blocks of time reminds us that sound investing is inherently long term in nature, and our planning will be wiser and more surely thought out when explicitly considered over the long, long term.

Of course, *planning* is only as useful as the actual *implementation* that follows. As was already noted, you will want to follow the wise coach's twin admonitions: "Plan your play, and play your plan."

The first step is clear: *Get out of debt.* It's a well-earned, great feeling when you achieve the first victory of paying off your school loans and the debts incurred while setting up your first household.

The key to getting out of debt is clear: Save! A lifetime based on the habit of thrift—spending less than you might and deferring the spending you do—is essential to saving. Those who assume or hope that their incomes will somehow outstrip their spending may believe in magic, but they are doomed to be disappointed, often grievously. "Pay yourself first" by putting money into savings on a regular basis. A dollar-cost-averaging account with a mutual fund, which automatically deducts a fixed dollar amount each month from your bank account or paycheck, is a good way to "pay yourself first."

There's a big difference between deliberate *borrowing* and *being in debt.* The *borrower* is comfortable because he or she has ample capacity to repay and, most important, decides or controls the timing of repayment. The *debtor* borrows only what a lender decides to lend—and must repay at the time chosen by the *lender.* That's why borrowing with a mortgage is very different from "being in debt." (Just as borrowing differs from being in debt, retirement differs from old age. In retirement you have more time for travel, reading, sports, and other interests. In old age your body aches in different ways *every* day. And every night.)

Figure 18-2 tells an important story about *inflation.* The figures in the second row, entitled "Nest-egg goal," are the amounts you would need to save by age 65 to have the inflation-adjusted equivalent of $35,000 in yearly spending money. (If you want $70,000 a year of spending money to sustain your lifestyle, multiply the figures in the second row by 2; if you want $105,000, multiply by 3, and so on.) Here's how to read the table:

- Find your present age in the top row.

- The *nest-egg goal* is the amount of capital you will need to accumulate to have an *inflation-adjusted* $35,000 to spend each year from age 65 on.

- The *current savings* on the left—ranging from $0 to $250,000—is the amount invested tax-free at a return of 10 percent annually until you reach age 65.

- The rest of the table shows how much you would need to save and invest each year to achieve your nest-egg goal.

- After retirement at age 65, the assumed returns average 7 percent. And at age 90, it is further assumed, all your accumulated savings will have been spent.

FIGURE 18-2   What it will take to get there from here.

Your current age	25	30	35	40	45	50	55
Nest-egg goal	$3 mil.	$2.5 mil.	$2.1 mil.	$1.7 mil.	$1.4 mil.	$1.1 mil.	$.94 mil.

Your current savings	How much you need to save annually						
$ 0	$6,890	$9,248	$12,524	$17,217	$24,300	$36,004	$58,995
$ 10,000	$5,868	$8,211	$11,463	$16,116	$23,125	$34,689	$57,367
$ 25,000	$4,334	$6,656	$ 9,872	$14,463	$21,363	$32,717	$54,926
$ 50,000	$1,777	$4,064	$ 7,220	$11,709	$18,427	$29,430	$50,857
$100,000	$ 0	$ 0	$ 1,916	$ 6,201	$12,554	$22,856	$42,720
$250,000	$ 0	$ 0	$ 0	$ 0	$ 0	$ 3,315	$18,308

Look at Figure 18-2 again. If you are age 30 (the second column), you'll need to accumulate *$2.5 million* when you reach age 65 to produce $35,000 a year of real spending money. The column shows—for each level of savings you've *already* accumulated—how much you'll have to save *every* year to achieve that goal.

Note the rather favorable assumptions: All your savings go into a tax-free account such as a 401(k) plan, where they are further assumed to compound at 10 percent annually until your retirement at age 65. In the future (starting from present market levels) this will be possible but not easy—even if you invest entirely in equities. In bonds, it simply cannot be done.

Remember algebra and solving equations with two unknowns? Did your course get to three unknowns? As investors, we are confronted by a much more complex challenge: to solve, or at least manage sensibly and rationally, a puzzle with *five* major unknowns, each of which is *changing*. The five unknowns are as follows:

- Rates of return on investments
- Inflation
- Spending
- Taxes
- Time

One analysis[1] of 35 years' experience (from 1964 to 2000) starts with the happy assumption that an investor retired in 1960 with a cool $1 million. The consequences of various investment programs are then examined. The *nominal* compound rates of return for this period were apparently quite encouraging: 11.8 percent for stocks, 7.9 percent for bonds, and 6.8 percent for Treasury bills (or cash equivalents). The very pleasing—but, as we'll soon see, very *deceptive*—theoretical final portfolio values produced by the initial $1 million after 35 years are as follows:

Stocks	$55.0 million
Bonds	$15.5 million
T-bills	$10.7 million

Everyone's a *winner!* Or so it may *appear.* But here's how the results look *after taxes:*

Stocks	$30.2 million
Bonds	$6.6 million
T-bills	$4.4 million

What a difference those taxes make—particularly to bonds and T-bills. Note that the taxes assumed are minimal: The investor pays only federal taxes (no state or local taxes), has no other sources of taxable income, and files a joint return. For most investors who can invest $1 million, actual taxes are almost certain to be larger.[2]

Brace yourself for the impact of *inflation,* because that's the way we convert *nominal* or *apparent* values into *real* money. The results are sobering. Here's the result after adjusting for inflation over the same 35 years:

Stocks	$5.4 million
Bonds	$1.2 million
T-bills	$0.8 million

Inflation is a far larger problem for investors than *taxes* are. In real purchasing power, bonds are only 20 percent ahead of the initial investment—

---

[1]Sanford C. Bernstein & Co. Inc., published in revised form in *The Journal of Investing,* Spring 1996, pp. 5–16.

[2] The effective tax rate on stocks is far lower than the effective tax rate on bonds because part of the return on stocks is market appreciation, and the capital gains tax rate is lower and payment often is deferred for many years—until you decide to sell. A reasonable estimate of the actual or effective federal tax rate on returns from stocks is about 20 percent, about half the tax rate on income from bonds or bills.

after a whole *generation*.[3] And T-bills are actually *behind* the starting line
by 20 percent. That's why taxes and inflation are rightly called "fearsome
fiscal pirates."

It would be worse if the study had included realistic ownership *costs*
such as mutual fund expenses and trading costs. Even the typical money
market mutual fund, a common way to manage cash, charges roughly 0.5
percent per year in expenses, while bond funds charge 1 percent and stock
funds charge around 1.4 percent. At those rates, you would have the following take-home results:

Stocks	$1.8 million
Bonds	$755,000
T-bills	$589,000

To earn the long-term "average" return, you would have been required
to have enough fortitude to stay fully invested when the market dropped
and inflation was tearing away at your portfolio (and your confidence *and*
determination to stay the course were faltering).

Spending is the next key factor. Again, time makes all the difference.
Consider the consequences of two commonly used spending rules. One
investor's rule is to limit spending to a moderate rate (such as 5 percent) of
your capital. If you followed this spending rule, as does Mr. 5 Percent, and
your investments were entirely in bonds, your $1 million would have fallen
in *real* money—or purchasing power—to just $200,000. The all-stock port-
folio alternative is, of course, better, but not by much. It would be up about
30 percent—less than 1 percent a *year*.

Another spending rule is to limit spending to cash income (that is, the
investor spends only the cash income of a stock portfolio) as dividends and
interest payments are received. This investor starts out having *less* to spend
than does Mr. 5 Percent but soon catches up and goes ahead in spending
more. Compounding is at work again.

Let's look behind the deceptive simplicity of the first of these two
widely accepted spending rules. "Five percent of capital" may be okay for
your alma mater, but colleges pay no taxes and can expect to receive future
contributions from alumni and others to help keep up with inflation. If you
know you won't live long, that *may* be okay for you, too. But if you live a
long time and spend a dollar amount equal to 5 percent of your original

---

[3]Note that in all but one year since 1950, if you invested in municipal bonds and then held
and reinvested for 20 years, you lost. In that one favorable initial investment year you made
0.01 percent annually after inflation, but before custody or management expenses.

capital and invest in bonds, your annual income from interest will be less than the 5 percent you'll be spending each year. Therefore, you'll have to invade capital to draw down the full 5 percent each year. The impact on your invested principal can be increasingly negative—at an accelerating rate—if your declining capital base is required to produce a higher and higher proportion of spendable funds to produce the 5 percent that originally appeared too moderate.

Beware of a subtle danger: An investor can almost always produce more income from a portfolio by investing more and more heavily in income stocks. But *other* investors are rational, and they'll let *you* get more today only if *they* can expect more tomorrow. Thus, part of what appears to be high current income is really a return of capital. (For example, so-called high-yield bonds may appear to pay, say, 8 to 10 percent interest, but part of that payment is actually a *return of capital*—the capital that's needed to off-set occasional, but probable, defaults.)

Money links the past with the present and the present with the future as a medium of stored value. You can estimate the dollars you'll want to spend each year and, at a spending rate such as 3 percent, the wealth required to produce the income to meet that level of spending. Determine what you have now and what you will save each year. Then see whether you can achieve your capital-accumulation objectives through a sensible investing program. If the first plan you design doesn't work out, you go around again: saving more each year *or* working and saving for more years *or* having less to live on. Be careful: Being optimistic will *not* help. Be cautious and conservative with each assumption: your saving rate, your rate of return, and your spending assumptions.

By combining your saving and capital *objectives* with your realistic *rate-of-return* expectations and your available *time horizon,* you can work out your own *investor's triangulation* to see what amount of capital or savings you will need to contribute each year to your long-term investments to be truly successful in achieving your realistic objectives for spendable money during retirement. (Your accountant or investment adviser can help you with the calculations.)

If you're surprised at how much you'll need to save and invest each year to meet retirement goals, it may be modestly comforting to know that you are not alone. Retirement is expensive partly because we live longer than did our parents or grandparents but primarily because inflation is such a powerful and unrelenting opponent.

For investors who do (or will) depend on their annual income from investments, the good news is that while interest paid on T-bills or bonds has fluctuated and will fluctuate (sometimes substantially) from year to year, dividends on a portfolio of common stocks will virtually never go down and will generally rise at approximately the rate of inflation.

Time is key in many ways. How long will you be saving? How long and how much will you be spending? How will the arrival of children, a new career, or a future illness change your spending and saving needs? How will investment opportunities differ over the years during which you invest? The careful study of investing history can be very useful to investors, but which history or which period of history should we study? After a wonderfully long and favorable market in America, there is a natural temptation to think the past 20 years are representative of history. They're not—any more than the beautiful days of summer define the climate of New England.

Investors may ponder the double-edged irony of death. If death comes sooner than expected and planned for, the resources saved over many years may go, at least partially, unused by the saver. If death comes much *later* than planned for, the saved-up resources may be too small, and grim poverty can result. Be prudent, but don't be prudent to excess. You *can* save too much, and those who love you do not want you to suffer a life of self-enforced poverty so that they can have extra money to spend after you're gone.

The best bargain for a long-term investor is to obtain sound investment counseling that leads to the sensible long-term investing program that is most appropriate to that investor. Ironically, most investors do not seek— and are unwilling to pay for—real help in developing an optimal long-term investment program. This grievous sin of omission incurs great *opportunity cost:* the cost of missing out on what might easily have been.

Ironically, most investors typically pay substantially more for such "implementing details" as investment management fees, stock brokerage commissions, and custody expenses than they would ever *consider* paying for overall investment counseling on their optimal long-term investment programs. To be specific, most investors could obtain very good investment counseling for a fee of less than $10,000 (paid only once each decade) and a sound estate plan for less than $20,000 (with 10-year modifications for less than $5,000).

Most investors would be unwilling to pay this much, yet the same individuals *will* regularly pay more than $10,000 per million dollars *every year* in investment operating expenses such as brokerage commissions, advisory fees, and custody expenses. It's ironic that investors will, however innocently, pay more for the lesser value.

Pick one day a year (for example, your birthday, New Year's Day, or

Thanksgiving) as *your* "day away for investing" and pledge to spend a quiet hour or so on that day every year quietly and systematically answering the following questions *in writing*. (After the first annual review, which may take several hours, you'll be updating the plan you wrote out *last* year, and so it won't take more than a few hours. You can make those few hours even more productive by rereading last year's plan a week or so *before* your "day away" so that it will be fresh in your mind and in your subconscious, where so much good thinking and rethinking can be done.) These questions will help define and articulate your objectives:

- During retirement, how much income do I want to have each year in addition to Social Security and my employer's pension benefit?

- How many years will I be in retirement? (The key here is to estimate how long you'll live. Ask your doctor how to apply the average life span of your parents or grandparents to get a reasonable fix on your own "genetic envelope," appropriately adjusted for the healthfulness of your personal lifestyle.)

- What spending rule am I ready to live with and live by?

- How much capital will I need to provide amply for retirement?

- After insurance, what capital will I need—inflation-adjusted—to cover full health care for my spouse and myself? (Your family doctor and local hospital can give you reasonable estimates based on their experience with people whose medical histories are similar to yours.)

- How much capital do I want to pass on to each member of my family and to any special friends?

- How much capital do I wish to direct to my philanthropic priorities?

Next comes an easy-to-use solution to what most investors consider the truly difficult part of the problem: estimating long-term average annual rates of return on your investments. Here's how:

- First, recognize that over the long, long term, *after adjusting for inflation,* average returns for each type of investment have been approximately as follows[4]:

---

[4]Precise figures for the 30 years from 1965 to 1994 *before* adjusting for the 5.4 percent inflation actually experienced: 6.7 percent for cash reserves, 7.0 percent for bonds, and 9.9 percent for stocks. (Courtesy of Ibbotson Associates.)

Stocks	4½ percent
Bonds	1½ percent
T-bills	1¼ percent

Thus, if you are operating on the assumption that you can get *real* returns of 10 percent a year from stocks, you are probably wrong.

- Second, comfortably in advance of your "annual day alone," ask representatives of three organizations this question in writing: "Over the past 20 years, the stock market's average annual total return has been *X* percent. Starting at the stock market's present price level, what average annual rate of return from today's market level would your firm expect over the *next* 20 years?" Next question: "Over the next 1-, 5-, and 20-year periods, what rate of inflation do you expect?" When you have their answers, take the *average* of their answers. (No, the result won't be precise, but it will be roughly accurate—and *useful*.) You'll now have two crucial estimates of the future: The nominal rate of return for the stock market and the amount you will have to adjust nominal returns to estimate the real (inflation-adjusted) rates of return.

- Third, remember and act on the understanding that over the truly long term the most important investment decisions seem almost obvious. Here are the two most important decision rules:

  Any funds that will stay invested for 10 years or longer should be in stocks.

  Any funds that will be invested for *less* than two to three years should be in "cash" or money market instruments.

Your next step is to prepare a complete inventory of your investment *assets,* including the following:

- Investments in stocks and bonds

- Equity in your home

- Assets in any retirement plans, including IRAs, Keoghs, and 401(k) or 403(b) plans

Over the long term benign neglect really does pay off.

Next, review your retirement income. (You can get help from your employer's human resources department or from your accountant.) Here are the obvious sources:

- Pension benefits

- Social Security

- Income from your investments

Next come your desired bequests to family members (and others) and intended charitable contributions.

In investing over the longer run benign neglect really does pay off. After basic decisions on long-term investment policy have been made with care and rigor, you should—with great respect—hold on to them. The problem, as Shakespeare put it, "lies not in our stars but in ourselves," so above all else, resist the insidious temptation to *do something.* "Nervous money never wins," say poker players. And they know. At Vail, the Kinderheim's experience-based sign offers a fine service at a great price: "Leave your kids for the day: $5." Then, mindful of past experience with overanxious parents, two "alternatives" are offered. "You *watch:* $10" and "You *help:* $25."

One final thought: Before making any commitments that are large in proportion to total wealth, the investor would be wise to reread *King Lear.*

19

ENDGAME

INVESTORS CAN—AND CERTAINLY SHOULD—substantially increase their lifetime financial and emotional success by paying appropriate attention to what chess players know is important: the *endgame.*

Deciding what will be done with your capital to maximize its real useful value can be just as important as deciding how to save, accumulate, and invest it. Providing for your retirement is one of three important challenges and opportunities. Bequests and gifts to those you love is another. The third—"giving back" to society—can be exciting and fulfilling.

Wealth *is* power—both the power to do good and the power to do harm. Greater wealth means greater power. Investors who have enjoyed substantial success should give careful consideration—no matter what their hopes or intentions—to whether the amount of wealth they can transfer to their children may do real harm by distorting their offspring's values and priorities or by taking away their descendants' joy of making their own way in life. It's well to recall Lord Acton's words: "Power tends to corrupt and absolute power corrupts absolutely." As we know, all too often poor little rich kids *are* miserable. While Mae West was speaking for herself when she announced that "too much of a good thing is *wunnerful,*" a large inheritance is not necessarily wonderful for your children. That's why Warren Buffet and Bill Gates have both announced that they'll give most of their money to charity.

Since money is such an effective way to store or transfer value, an investor with a surplus beyond his or her own lifetime's wants and needs will have the opportunity to make a difference to others. Blessed is the investor whose assets do *good;* cursed are those who, despite their best intentions, cause *harm.*

A large inheritance is not necessarily wonderful for your children.

Before outlining some of the possibilities for transfers within the circle of those you love or feel responsibility for, let's remember that money has powerful symbolic meaning. Psychiatrists marvel that while patients talk rather extensively and relatively early in therapy about relationships with parents, childhood experiences, central hopes and fears, and even normally very private matters such as dreams and sexual experiences, the one subject almost never discussed is *money.*

Most people find it very difficult to discuss money matters openly, fully, rationally, and wisely. Therefore, it's best to be especially thoughtful and cautious when making plans about how your money will pass to others. Yes, it's your money now and while you live—but neither of these cheerful current realities is forever. Money is the thermonuclear device among symbols: It symbolizes a *lot*—in different ways for different people, often in quite unexpected ways.

You'll want to get expert legal advice when formulating a sound estate plan, but here are some items for consideration, recognizing that each person will have his or her own objectives and resources and will want to make his or her own decisions:

1. Everyone who qualifies for an individual retirement account (IRA) should have one. And everyone who can possibly afford to do so should contribute the (now $2,000) maximum every year, enabling the twin engines of long-term compounding and tax deferral to do their magic.

    Get your children or grandchildren started early. You can give an IRA contribution of up to $2,000 per year to each child or grandchild up to the amount of their earned income each year.

2. You can give up to $10,000—without tax—to *each* person you wish *every* year. Married couples can give $20,000 annually to each person. For most investors these annual gifts can over time be a central, even dominant part of a lifelong estate planning and family investment managing program. (Gifts to young children

can be made in care of a parent as custodian under the Uniform Transfers to Minors Act.)

You might concentrate on your children. Such gifts can really mount up (partly because the future investment income earned on the sums given is taxed at the child's tax rate, which is almost certain to be far lower than yours). Over 20 years, $10,000 given annually can, with sensible investing, accumulate to the better part of $500,000.

The main advantage of these gifts lies in completely sidestepping the estate tax when you die. Again, the keys to success are *time* and *compounding,* so plan well, start early, and stay with your plan.

3. You have a lifetime limit of $1 million on other tax-free gifts to individuals. A serious look at estate tax tables—particularly at the highest incremental rate you're likely to incur—will strongly encourage you to use this right to give. And contemplation of the cumulative consequences of compound interest will encourage you to use this right relatively early in life.

4. Despite the Elizabethan laws against "perpetuities," the IRS allows you to put up to $1 million into a generation-skipping tax-free family fund. (Your children can decide how their trust's assets will be divided among your descendants.) Gift or estate taxes must be paid before the assets pass to this fund. However, once this initial tax is paid, the assets can grow and accumulate in a gift, estate, and generation-skipping tax-free environment for several generations within your family, typically for up to 80 to 100 years. Remember that if investments increase 7 percent per annum after income tax, they will double every 10 years, and $1 million will become $1 billion in 100 years. In the meantime, this family fund can operate as a family bank by allowing distributions or loans to family members as needed. Wealthy investors should consider this option.

5. A curious provision called a qualified personal residence trust enables you to transfer ownership of your house to your children and live in your home rent-free for a period of time (such as 15 years). You save substantially on estate taxes—unless you die before the trust matures—while ownership passes to your children.

For example, a $1 million home can be transferred as a taxable gift valued at only 20 to 30 percent of the current market value for this reason: The IRS considers the taxable *present* value of the gift to be *only* the value of the children's right to take possession at the end of the 15-year term of the trust. (The discount to a low present value is the obverse of the powerful accumulation or growth generated by compound interest.)

Money symbolizes a lot—in different ways for different people.

6. If you wish to transfer substantial sums to your descendants but worry about distorting their values and lives with too much money at too early an age—before they reach "fiscal maturity"—consider an arrangement used by Jackie Onassis.[1]

    Here's the general idea: A trust can be established for 20 to 30 years with interim annual distributions of income payable to your favorite school or charity (either at a set dollar amount or as a percentage of the trust's assets)—with the trust *corpus*[2] paid after the 20- to 30-year term to the chosen beneficiaries. There's no estate tax, and a gift tax is paid only on the estimated net present value of the trust's corpus after discounting at the IRS's prescribed interest rate, an amount that is only a fraction of the probable market value of the corpus 20 to 30 years from now.

    If you are concerned about the harm that might be done by a *current* wealth transfer to a 30- to 35-year-old beneficiary but are sanguine that the same transfer in the *future* would not harm the values of that person at age 60 or 65, this sort of trust can be an effective way to transfer substantial wealth with minimal tax. (Noting that the key figures are all based on long-term *estimates* of market valuations far in the future, the wise investor will want to work out the specific term of the trust and the investment policy under several different scenarios and select the choice with which he or she feels most confident and comfortable.)

7. Curiously, and quite accurately, estate lawyers will advise that one of the best assets to use for charitable giving at your death may be your currently *tax-exempt* defined contribution retirement fund: 401(k), 403(b), IRA, or profit-sharing plan.

---

[1]But reversed by her children under an optional provision in her will.

[2]The principal, or main body, of the money, from the Latin word for "body."

This surprising anomaly is true because these assets must be included in your estate. And this means not only that you incur the estate tax but that you also incur income taxes as distributions are paid to beneficiaries on your date of death. However, both of these taxes can be avoided if you decide to donate the capital to charity.

Inverted or upside-down reasoning can be a usefully mind-freeing way to explore any complex issue. Investors can think of estate taxes not as a tax on *wealth* but as a tax on your reluctance to make irrevocable decisions while living (particularly long, long before your death) about the distribution of your wealth. *If* you are willing and able to make irrevocable decisions *now* regarding the long-term future disposition of your capital, you can save substantially on taxes. As Ben Franklin said, "A penny saved is a penny earned."

Most investors are *not* willing to make these wealth-distribution decisions. But please remember, the power of compound interest can be used for the maximum period to have the maximum impact on achieving your carefully considered goals and objectives *only* if you are willing to make decisions about the future now.

Maximizing your lifetime financial success has five stages or dimensions:

- Earning
- Saving
- Investing
- Contributing
- Estate planning

Ideally, you will maximize achievement in each area along your own value dimensions within the feasible set of opportunities available to you as you enjoy a full and balanced life.

Investors who have conscientiously worked to *maximize* the amount of their savings and investments will want to pay comparable attention to *minimizing* the diversion of funds caused by taxes, particularly estate taxes. This effort will maximize the amount of funds devoted to achieving your desired fiscal objectives.

If you have surplus funds beyond the amount you wish to transfer to members of your family and others you care for, don't overlook the profoundly rewarding opportunities you may have created for yourself to cause good things to happen.

"Giving money away to charity" puts the whole proposition the wrong way. Instead, think in terms of imaginatively and vigorously *using* your money—the stored values you and your skills have created over many years—to make good things happen for and through the people and organizations you care about. You can derive a great deal of pleasure and personal fulfillment in the process of making a positive difference in people's lives.

Think of your money as the stored values that you and your skills have created.

Select the actions or changes that would give you deep spiritual satisfaction or pleasure to see coming to fruition. You make these good things come true by committing capital to help *make* them happen. Like many others, you may find gratification in converting your financial resources into actions and values you truly care about. After all, your financial resources are the stored-up consequences of your hard work, imagination, and good fortune. Here are some opportunities to make an impact:

- Establish scholarships for young people with great talent who aspire to make significant contributions in the arts, science, or business.

- Contribute to scholarships for young people who've gotten a bad deal in life and need someone's help to get on the right road. (If you don't have a particular school in mind, consider Berea College, which accepts *only* kids who can't afford a college education.)

- Provide financial support for science or medicine or social justice.

- Support hospitals, shelters, and other institutions to help those in severe need.

- Help make your community a better place to live in by being one of the "go-to" leaders who commit time and money to make good things happen.

- Supply funding for the arts—music, dance, or theater—that enrich our lives.

Your greatest satisfaction may come from serving a major national institution, a global organization, or a small entity in your neighborhood. Experienced charitable activists agree that while contributing money *is* important, even greater enjoyment and satisfaction accrue when you also make a substantial commitment of your time, skill, and energy. Don't leave this important part of your life experience "in storage" in the attic or the bank—or for someone else to enjoy doing. Look around. Get involved through an active, long-term program of strategic giving.

Contributors have learned how greatly they can enjoy seeing the wealth they have created—through years of adding economic value in their working years by producing and delivering better services and products—come to life yet *again* by reducing constraints on individuals or society and enabling good things to happen during their lives in ways that matter to them. As the old saying has it, "You can't take it with you." Those who give something back invariably speak of this dimension of their lives with genuine satisfaction. And those who contribute *more* find they enjoy even *greater* satisfaction.[3]

Contributing your time, talent, and money can be profoundly rewarding in two ways. For yourself, there is great personal satisfaction in seeing how real, living people and organizations benefit. And very satisfying personal experiences result from engaging productively with stimulating and interesting people and making new and valuable friendships.

As with other areas of investing, it's wise to plan ahead, to be conservative (within limits), and to make productive use of time by beginning early and sustaining your commitments over as long a period as you can provide yourself.[4]

---

[3]One of my personal "lightbulbs" lit up while I was enjoying clams at Charley O's restaurant in Rockefeller Center in 1974. Huge black-and-white photographs of movie stars decorated the walls; each had a one-line quote under the picture. The movie star looming over my table was the once very dissolute Tasmanian swashbuckler Errol Flynn. His quote: "Any guy who dies with more than 10 grand has made a mistake." While Flynn surely had other things on his mind, I resolved there and then to avoid the mistake of paying more than necessary in estate taxes by giving during my lifetime. I prefer to make some errors of *commission* (giving to causes that later disappoint) than to make errors of *omission* (giving too little or too late). It's been interesting and fun—and very rewarding.

[4]Claude Rosenberg, in addition to authoring several good books on how to make money in investing, has written *Wealthy and Wise,* a pioneering book on how to think through what you can afford to contribute.

C H A P T E R

20

YOU ARE NOW GOOD TO GO!

YOU—NOT YOUR PROFESSIONAL investment managers—have the most important job in successful investment management. Your central responsibilities are to decide on your long-term investment objectives and, with the expert advice of professional managers, determine a well-reasoned and realistic set of investment policies that can achieve those objectives.

Only by separating responsibility for investment *policy* from responsibility for portfolio *operations* can you delegate to a manager the authority to implement policy in daily portfolio operations without abdicating your responsibility for defining your objectives and making sure that investment policies are designed to achieve your chosen objectives.

The great purpose of investment policy is to provide sound guidance, particularly when market conditions are the most distressing and create the most urgent anxiety about the true wisdom of that policy.

You should study your total investment situation, your emotional tolerance of risk, and the history of investment markets, because a mismatch between the market's sometimes grim realities and your financial and emotional needs can result—and has resulted—in great harm.

Investors who study the realities of investing will be able to protect themselves and their investments from the all too common but unrealistic belief that they can find portfolio managers who will substantially "beat the market." The well-informed investor understands that the only way an active investment manager can beat the market is to find and exploit other investors' mistakes more often than they find and exploit his mistakes and that a manager who strives to beat the market is all too likely to try too hard and be beaten instead. Most of the managers and clients who insist on trying, either on their own or with professional managers, will be disappointed by the results. It *is* a Loser's Game.

Happily, there is an easy way to win the Loser's Game—simply by *not playing,* or at least not playing by the conventional rules that are so out of date. As George Marshall counseled his senior officers on the way to win World War II: "Don't fight the problem." Accept reality. As expert card players advise, "Play your hand as it lays." Tommy Armour, the great golf instructor, wisely advised, "Hit the shot that makes the next shot easy!"

Times have changed. Even as the old ways of managing portfolios to beat the market have become obsolete, a new approach has become available— and it works. It downplays portfolio *operations*, particularly of the heroic variety, and concentrates on carefully thought through, well-documented, and well-defined long-term investment *policy*.

Recognizing that higher returns are the incentive and reward for investors taking—and sustaining—modestly above-average market risk and that the highest returns therefore come from equity investments, you should set your portfolio's asset mix at the highest ratio of equities that your economic and emotional limitations can sustain over the long term.

To do your work well, you must understand the turbulent nature of markets in the short term and the basic consistency of markets in the long term. This understanding will enable you to increase your tolerance for interim market fluctuations while you concentrate on the long-term purpose of the portfolio, taking full advantage of any investor's greatest resource: time.

Some losing is an everyday reality: Stock prices go up and down daily. Inflation corrodes the purchasing power value of investments day after day. The challenge—and the opportunity—is to never lose *big*.

Raised in the tradition that says, "If you find a problem, find a solution," I felt intrigued by the task of finding a solution to the problem identified long ago in "The Loser's Game."[1] As is often true, the solution was to "think outside the box" and *redefine* the problem. Thus, my focus shifted from the Loser's Game (working even harder in a futile effort to beat the

---

[1]Written in 1975 for the *Financial Analyst Journal,* where it won the profession's Graham Dodd Award.

market) to a winner's game of concentrating on the big picture of longer-term asset mix and investment policy—and *staying the course*.

Individual investors are important to me for three major reasons. First, there are so many of them, nearly 50 million in the United States and almost as many in other nations; second, almost all individual investors are truly "on their own" in designing long-term investment policies and strategies because there are few investment consultants who can afford to provide the counseling individuals need at a reasonable fee; and third, virtually all how-to books on investing are sold on the false promise that the typical individual can beat the professional investors. She can't and she won't.

And the individual investor does not have to. Successful investing does not depend on beating the market. Attempting to "beat the market"—to do better than other investors—will distract you from the fairly simple but interesting and productive task of designing a long-term program of investing that *will succeed* at providing the best feasible results for you.

If you feel, as I do, that some of the advice in this book is pretty simple, please keep in mind the observation of two of my best friends, who are at the peak of their distinguished careers in medicine and medical research. They agree that the two most important discoveries in medical history are penicillin and washing the hands (which stopped the spreading of infection from one mother to another by the midwives who delivered most babies before 1900). What's more, my friends counsel, there's no better advice on how to live longer than to quit smoking and to buckle up when driving. The lesson: Advice doesn't have to be complicated to be good.

Soundly conceived, persistently followed long-term investment policy *is* the pathway to success in investing. The actions required are not complicated. The real challenge is to commit to the discipline of long-term investing and avoid the compelling distractions of the excitement that surrounds, but is superfluous to, the real work of investing. This commitment to the discipline of long-term investing is your principal responsibility—and opportunity to contribute. Winning the Loser's Game of beating the market is easy: *don't play it.* Concentrate on the winner's game: defining and adhering faithfully to sound investment policy that's right for the market realities and right for your long-term goals and objectives.

Despite the fact that everybody "knows" that each family's funds—and each pension fund or endowment fund—differs in situation from every other fund (and that these differences are often substantial), and despite the conventional consensus that these substantial differences should be reflected in different investment policies and practices, the fact is that the investment portfolios of most funds are very much alike.

This is not the way it should be. The needs and purposes of investors are not the same, and their investment portfolios should not be the same. Also, the relationships between managers and clients are not and should not be the same. Some clients are sophisticated experts; others are not. As clients' knowledge differs, their relationship with managers should differ.

Without clear direction from clients, it is natural for investment managers to move toward the center, to put portfolios in neutral, to be conventional. (It is also easier to treat all investors the same.) Therefore, investment managers will tend to produce average portfolios for *all* their clients rather than portfolios that are carefully designed to meet the particular objectives of each individual investor.

At the same time, ironically, professional investment managers lament over and over again that they feel they must compromise their investment decisions because clients do not do their part. In particular, managers believe they could achieve far better results if their clients took a longer-term view of the investment process and would be more specific about the kind of investment portfolio they really want.

Clients "own" the central responsibility for formulating—and assuring the implementation of—long-term investment policy. This responsibility cannot be delegated to investment managers; it is *your* job, not theirs. Fortunately, this client responsibility can be fulfilled without extensive experience in the operational complexities of contemporary securities analysis or portfolio management.

To fulfill your responsibilities to yourself, you need three characteristics: (1) a genuine interest in developing an understanding of your true interests and objectives, (2) an appreciation of the fundamental nature of capital markets and investments, including Mr. Market's clever tricks, and (3) the discipline to work out and hold on to the basic policies that will over time succeed in fulfilling your realistic investment objectives. That's what this book is about.

Professional investment managers should encourage their clients to use this book as a guide to performing the vital role of being informed, active, and therefore *successful* clients.

While it is a spirited critique of contemporary investment practice, this book is by no means a condemnation of investment managers. The problem is not that professional managers lack skill or diligence. Quite the opposite. The problem with trying to beat the market is that professional investors are so talented, numerous, and dedicated to their work that as a group they make it very difficult for any one of their number to do significantly better than the others, particularly in the long run.

There are two different kinds of problems in trying to beat the market. One problem is that this is extraordinarily difficult to do—and easy, while trying to do better, to do *worse*. The other problem with trying to "beat the market" as your primary investment objective is that you will divert both your own attention and that of your investment manager from the need to establish long-range objectives and investment policies that are well matched to your particular needs.

The real purpose of investment management is not to "beat the market" but to do what is right for a particular client.

Do investors matter? They *should*, but you will matter only if you assert your authority and fulfill these responsibilities: deciding on investment objectives, developing sound investment policies, and holding your portfolio managers accountable for implementing long-term investment policy in daily portfolio operations.

This book is written with a clear point of view: Investors all too often delegate—or, more accurately, abdicate—to their investment managers responsibilities which they can and should keep for themselves. Their undelegatable responsibilities are setting explicit investment policies consistent with their objectives, defining long-range objectives appropriate to their particular fund, and managing their managers to ensure that their policies are being followed.

This book is a guide for those who will accept this central client responsibility and want to be successful at achieving their true and realistic objectives.

Much as it might seem obvious that client investors should care a lot about the way their money is managed, the reality is they typically do almost nothing about it—until it's too late. In short, this book is written for investors who are prepared to take charge of their own investment destiny.

You now know all you will ever need to know to be truly successful with investments—as a successful *client* of professional investment managers. You are now ready to enjoy *winning investing*. You're good to go!

PARTING
THOUGHTS

OUBT," SAID THE PHYSICIST RICHARD FEYNMAN, "is the necessary first step toward creativity." I've learned to double-check my answers, particularly when the evidence seems most confirming, and ask, "Could I be wrong?" Basic to all you've read here are certain structural realities that are not going to change:

- The number of brilliant, hardworking professionals is not going to decrease, certainly not enough to convert investing back into the winner's game of the 1960s.

- The proportion of transactions controlled by institutions—and the splendid professionals who lead them—will not decline. Investing will stay dangerous.

- Maybe some day so many investors will agree to index that the last guys standing will have the opportunity to have the field all to themselves. That'll be the day.

Be sure to call me when these things happen. Meanwhile, I've got better things to do—where I can play to win with both my time and my money. And so do you.

If you wish to read more, as I hope you will, here are 10 choices you'll find both enjoyable and very worthwhile.

1. *Berkshire Hathaway Annual Reports.* Warren Buffett, who is rec-
    ognized as our most successful investor, explains with humor and
    candor what he and Charlie Munger are doing and why. Delightful
    as recreational reading and profoundly instructive for profession-
    als, these remarkable annual reports are an open classroom for
    investors. The justly famous annual meetings of Berkshire's stock-
    holders are equally candid, entertaining, and informative. Current
    and past years' reports are available over the Internet.

2. *The Intelligent Investor* by Benjamin Graham, the acknowledged
    founder of the profession of investment management. This is an
    "advanced primer" and the only investment book endorsed by
    Warren Buffett, who once worked for Graham. (If you want more
    depth, breadth, and rigor, turn to *Security Analysis,* which is often
    called Graham and Dodd after its authors. For 70 years, through
    six editions, it has been the professional investor's bible.)

3. *Bogle on Investing.* Jack Bogle is the tribune for the individual
    investor, the founder of Vanguard, and a crusader with the odd but
    delightful quirk of thinking clearly, writing well, and having a lot
    to say that we should all treasure and use.

4. *Pioneering Portfolio Management.* David Swensen, Yale's very
    successful chief investment officer, explains how to manage a
    large tax-exempt portfolio in a thoroughly modern way with no
    jargon, no complex equations, and lots of good thinking and judg-
    ment. Fully accessible to serious amateurs, this is the best book
    ever written about professional investing.

5. *Why Smart People Make Big Money Mistakes—and How to Cor-
    rect Them* by Gary Belsky and Thomas Gilovich. This is an engag-
    ing, easy read about how and why we blunder with money
    decisions *and* how to defend ourselves against ourselves and our
    all too human proclivities.

6. *The Crowd* by Gustave LeBon. This book shows that intelligent
    people lose their rationality and individuality when they join
    groups or, worse, become part of a crowd. Investors exhibit
    "crowd behavior" all too often.

7. *The Only Investment Book You'll Ever Need* by Andrew Tobias of
    Fortune. This is a primer without any patronizing. It is clear, com-
    prehensive, candid, and charming.

8. *A Random Walk down Wall Street* by Burton Malkiel. Soon to sell
    its millionth copy, this popular guide to what the professionals

know—and should know—provides straight talk from one of Princeton's favorite professors.

9. *An Investor's Anthology* is a collection of justly famous insights and ideas that "ring the bell" for professional investors. Seminal papers of great influence that are abstruse or opaque were deliberately excluded.

10. *Wealthy and Wise* is Claude Rosenberg's thoughtfully challenging explanation of how to recognize how much of your wealth and income you could reinvest in philanthropy and thereby enrich your life.

Some of the best writing and thinking about investing comes in articles written by five journalists. I try to read everything they write:

Jonathan Clements of *The Wall Street Journal*
Carol Loomis of *Fortune*
Floyd Norris of *The New York Times*
Barry Riley of *The Financial Times*
Jason Zweig of *Money*

ABOUT THE AUTHOR

Charles D. Ellis served for 28 years as managing partner of Greenwich Associates, the global leader in strategy consulting to professional financial service firms, and has consulted with the world's leading investment managers and securities firms primarily in the United States but also in Australia, Canada, Japan, and the United Kingdom. The author of 10 books and nearly 100 articles on investing, Ellis has taught investment courses at the Harvard Business School and the Yale School of Management. In addition to chairing AIMR (the investment management profession's worldwide association), he has served as a trustee of Phillips Exeter Academy, an overseer of the Stern Schools of Business at New York University, a director of the Harvard Business School, and is a trustee of the Whitehead Institute for Biomedical Research and a successor trustee of Yale University, where he chairs the investment committee.

INDEX